D0115527

The American History Series
Series Editors
John Hope Franklin, *Duke University*
Abraham S. Eisenstadt, *Brooklyn College*

Arthur S. Link
Princeton University
General Editor for History

Alan M. Kraut
THE AMERICAN UNIVERSITY

The Huddled Masses:
The Immigrant in American Society, 1880–1921

Harlan Davidson, Inc.
Arlington Heights, Illinois 60004

Library of Congress Cataloging in Publication Data

Kraut, Alan M.
    The huddled masses.

    (The American history series)
    Bibliography: p.
    Includes index.
    1. United States—Emigration and immigration—History.
2. Americanization—History. I. Title. II. Series:
American history series (Harlan Davidson, Inc.)
JV6450.K7   304.8′73   81-17488
ISBN 0-88295-810-0   AACR2

Cover design: Roger Eggers

Cover illustration: Charles Frederic Ulrich, *In the Land of Promise—Castle Garden,* in the Collection of The Corcoran Gallery of Art, Museum Purchase, Gallery Fund.

Manufactured in the United States of America
90 89 88 87 86 MA 5 6 7 8 9 10 11

For my parents,
Jeanette and Harry Kraut

EDITORS' FOREWORD

Every generation writes its own history, for the reason that it sees the past in the foreshortened perspective of its own experience. This has certainly been true of the writing of American history. The practical aim of our historiography is to offer us a more certain sense of where we are going by helping us understand the road we took in getting where we are. If the substance and nature of our historical writing is changing, it is precisely because our own generation is redefining its direction, much as the generations that preceded us redefined theirs. We are seeking a newer direction, because we are facing new problems, changing our values and premises, and shaping new institutions to meet new needs. Thus, the vitality of the present inspires the vitality of our writing about our past. Today's scholars are hard at work reconsidering every major field of our history: its politics, diplomacy, economy, society, mores, values, sexuality, and status, ethnic, and race relations. No less significantly, our scholars are using newer modes of investigation to probe the ever-expanding domain of the American past.

Our aim, in this American History Series, is to offer the reader a survey of what scholars are saying about the central themes and issues of American history. To present these themes and issues, we have invited scholars who have made notable contributions to the respective fields in which they are writing. Each volume offers the reader a sufficient factual and narrative account for perceiving the larger dimensions of its particular subject. Addressing their respective themes, our authors have undertaken, moreover, to present the conclusions derived by the principal writers on these themes. Beyond that, the authors present their own conclusions about those aspects of their respective subjects that have been matters of difference and controversy. In effect, they have written not only about where the subject stands in today's historiography but also about where they stand on their subject. Each volume closes with an extensive critical essay on the writings of the major authorities on its particular theme.

The books in this series are designed for use in both basic and advanced courses in American history. Such a series has a particular utility in times such as these, when the traditional format of our American history courses is being altered to accommodate a greater diversity of texts and reading materials. The series offers a number of distinct advantages. It extends and deepens the dimensions of course work in American history. In proceeding beyond the confines of the traditional textbook, it makes clear that the study of our past is, more than the student might otherwise infer, at once complex, sophisticated, and profound. It presents American history as a subject of continuing vitality and fresh investigation. The work of experts in their respective fields, it opens up to the student the rich findings of historical inquiry. It invites the student to join, in major fields of research, the many groups of scholars who are pondering anew the central themes and problems of our past. It challenges the student to participate actively in exploring American history and to collaborate in the creative and rigorous adventure of seeking out its wider reaches.

John Hope Franklin

Abraham S. Eisenstadt

ACKNOWLEDGMENTS

Even short volumes incur long lists of debts. Harlan Davidson as well as editors Abraham Eisenstadt and John Hope Franklin were patient despite the repeated delays that tried their fortitude as much as the author's. Abe Eisenstadt's guidance and the suggestions of two anonymous readers helped the author to improve the final version. Joel H. Silbey introduced me to the ethnocultural interpretation of mass voting behavior as a graduate student and thereby nurtured my interest in the influence of race, religion, and ethnicity in American society. Louis Joughin generously shared with me his data and expertise on the Sacco-Vanzetti case as well as his many astute perceptions of American attitudes toward immigrants in the 1920s. I am also especially indebted to my colleagues and students at The American University. Robert L. Beisner and Allan J. Lichtman read and discussed with me my early drafts. Kay Mussell and Janet Oppenheim served as excellent sounding boards for ideas. My graduate students helped considerably. Sarah Larson, already a talented writer, provided invaluable editorial assistance and co-authored the photographic essay. Melissa Kirkpatrick read drafts and assisted with the indexing of the manuscript. My undergraduate students at A.U. and the many foreign scholars whom I have addressed at the Washington International Center asked the questions to which this book is a response. Vivian Hogan typed the final draft with speed and good humor. My wife, Deborah, encouraged me to write this book because she has always preferred the second half of the nineteenth century to the first. She read my drafts, some of them; she criticized my prose, always; and she sent out for Chinese food when hunger got the best of us both. Most of all, her affection sustained me. My daughter, Julia Rose, was born months after the manuscript was completed and yet, for various reasons, she has had more to do with this volume than almost anyone else. Even as I write these words she is perched atop my desk. I await the day when she can read this book and criticize any errors in it for which her father quite properly accepts full responsibility.

CONTENTS

The land flourished because it was fed from so many sources—
because it was nourished by so many cultures and traditions and
peoples.

Lyndon Baines Johnson
October 3, 1965

Introduction

On the chilly, foggy afternoon of October 28, 1886, the Statue
of Liberty was unveiled by its sculptor, August Bartholdi. The
151-foot copper statue had been a gift from France to the United
States in celebration of the American centennial in 1876. Now, a
decade later, it was complete, mounted atop a 150-foot concrete
pedestal on Bedloe's Island in the New York Harbor. The ceremony was given over to speeches, most of them praising Franco-
American relations and the principles of democracy. President
Grover Cleveland and other speakers remarked on international
goodwill and peace and the beneficial influence that American
political ideals could have on nations throughout the world.

Ironically, at the tip of Manhattan, within view of Bedloe's Island, foreigners were crowding off boats, anxious to partake of American ideals and opportunities. That Liberty might be raising her giant torch in welcome to the immigrants did not occur to most of those who addressed the crowd in 1886. Only Emma Lazarus had envisioned the statue as a beacon to those arriving from foreign shores. In a poem written in 1883, "The New Colossus," she imagined the monument issuing a dramatic invitation to the world's nations:

> Give me your tired, your poor,
> Your huddled masses yearning to breathe free,
> The wretched refuse of your teeming shore,
> Send these, the nameless, tempest-tost to me,
> I lift my lamp beside the golden door!

Lazarus' verse, written to help raise money for the statue's pedestal, received merely polite applause at the dedication ceremony. Only years later would the general public come to share her understanding of the statue's symbolic importance.

"Huddled masses" by the millions had already been landing in America since the 1850s, but an even greater number would come in the decades after Liberty assumed her vigil in New York Harbor. Immigration ceased only temporarily with the turmoil of the Civil War. Prior to the war, most immigrants to the United States were emigrating from northern and western Europe. However, beginning in the early 1880s the main sources of immigrants shifted to southern Europe and eastern Europe; nations such as Italy, Greece, Russia, Lithuania, Latvia, and the smaller Balkan states. By 1907, over 80 percent of the 1,285,000 immigrants reaching the United States were from these countries, as compared to only 13 percent in 1882. Meanwhile, within this hemisphere hundreds of thousands of French Canadians from the north and Mexicans from the south crossed America's borders, often without even formally registering their presence. Between 1880 and 1921, over 23,500,000 people took advantage of America's lenient immigration policies and came to the United States. They came to be called the "new immigrants."

Emma Lazarus' vivid imagery of those newcomers as "huddled," "wretched," "tempest-tost," travelers awash on the shores of America is compelling. It has stirred the souls of many authors and has inspired the titles of countless books. However, while historians have pressed beyond this moving and poetic image, best exemplified by Oscar Handlin's haunting portrait in *The Uprooted* (1951), to a fuller more complex analysis of migration and migrant, the popular mind has lagged behind. The general reader, informed by journalists, television producers, and politicians, clings to a simplistic and distorted image of the newcomers. Immigrants are romanticized as heroes and heroines bravely overcoming all obstacles to reach an America they intuitively knew would be a better home; or they are pitied as bedraggled wayfarers, expelled from their homelands by vast social forces beyond their comprehension or control, driven to emigrate and attracted to America by the blandishments of profit-seeking land agents and entrepreneurs.

Once in America, so the story goes, plucky immigrants ascended from rags to riches through perseverance and will, or were broken—harassed by American immigration officials, trapped within the poverty and squalor of urban industrial life, exploited in mines, factories, and sweatshops. According to this interpretation, America's unparalleled economic growth provided the newcomers with incredible opportunities, provided they submerged themselves in American society and abandoned the cultural legacies of their homelands.

Increasingly, historians have come to reject any simplistic, monolithic pattern of race and ethnicity. No longer do scholars treat all immigrants collectively as history's dissatisfied masses who hoped to escape their problems by flight. Nor do they insist that members of each racial or religious group all shared like motives for emigration. There are fewer casual references to "the Italians," "the Poles," or "the Jews" as if these subgroups were homogeneous in values, beliefs, and behavior. There remains, however, a neglect of the individual immigrant. Too often, still, historians fail adequately to acknowledge that it was the single individual who decided to go or stay. The immigrant might not always have been the sole arbiter of his or her own fate, but neither was the immigrant primarily a passive soul, reactive and compliant before impersonal social forces. Weak, beaten men and women do not undertake transoceanic journeys to far-off lands unless they are herded aboard ship at gunpoint.

Wise in the world's ways, most immigrants knew that there was a price tag attached to every decision, even if the cost was for the moment indecipherable. And for many people, the price of emigration was too high compared with that of other options. For an east European Jew or Slavic peasant, emigrating to America was not the only means to a better life. One could learn new skills, move to a neighboring country or one in western Europe, change occupations, migrate to another region of one's own country, or pursue the struggle in place, hoping to earn enough to offer the next generation a better start in life's competition. The majority of the people in southern and eastern Europe—people who did *not* leave for America—are evidence that such an array of choices existed.

This study contends that portraits of the newcomer as the clever calculator of New World opportunity, or the passive, reactive object of others' decisions are equally exaggerated and unrealistic. Such portrayals miss the subtlety and complexity of the immigrant experience and diminish the humanity of each man and woman who opted to seek his or her fortune abroad. This is not to say, however, that each immigrant's odyssey was thoroughly unique. Interviews with some immigrants and the letters and memoirs of others suggest a web of factors that in varied measure influenced those who uprooted themselves. Four considerations emerge as crucial, both in the decision to depart for the New World and in the reaction to American society. These are: (1) the historical experience of the new immigrant's ethnic group; (2) the cultural values of that group; (3) the immigrant's own goals and expectations; and (4) his or her individual abilities and aptitudes. Almost always, these four considerations, separately or in combination, formed the immigrant's decisions and reactions.

The time is long gone when immigrants from diverse societies and cultures can be discussed collectively as if they were the same except for their quaint native garb. Throughout this volume, therefore, special pains have been taken to distinguish the choices made by members of different national and cultural groups. No immigrant arrived tabula rasa. Each newcomer sifted his decisions through a filter of experiences and perceptions unique to his group, as well as those unique to his person.

This book combines general description of the new immigration with an analysis of the different aspects of new immigrant life in America. Though the designation "new immigrant" referred to southern and eastern Europeans only, this volume includes the Chinese and Japanese who arrived in the period from 1880 to 1921. Both groups, though small in number, were as culturally different as the other new immigrant groups from the northern and western European voyagers of an earlier era. Moreover, Asian immigrants, especially those who settled on the Pacific Coast, faced obstacles equal to, if not greater than, those of their European counterparts.

Likewise, Mexicans and French Canadians had crossed America's borders long before the 1880s. However, during the late nineteenth century, this immigration was sharply stepped up. Clustering in towns and small cities, these immigrants had a significant impact upon the southwest and northeast and cannot be ignored in studies of this era.

Chapter One begins by placing the new immigration into a broad perspective as just one phase of a larger westward migration taking place in nineteenth-century Europe. Seen in this light, the migration to America becomes a conscious choice made by immigrants among several practical alternatives, rather than the result of an almost mystical allure that drew immigrants through the "golden door."

The second chapter describes admission procedures at American immigration depots; for most, the first contact with their new home. The immigrant is followed through a typical landing and inspection at Ellis Island, the nation's largest and busiest reception center. The remainder of the chapter discusses the crucial first decision of immigrants: where to reside in this vast, unfamiliar country. Immigrant communities were not established by accident or fiat, but by the desire of their residents. Most immigrants chose to live in cities or large towns, but a handful did opt for smaller towns in rural communities.

The newcomer's decision where to live was often related to choice of occupation and attitude toward economic advancement. Chapter Three suggests that the various immigrants' occupational choices were product of old-world experiences and cultural values, the intention to settle permanently or return to the native land, and uniquely individual talents and attitudes. Different immigrant groups achieved material prosperity and social prestige at different rates, albeit over the same routes. These differences resulted from the unique cultural priorities of particular groups. Not all immigrants shared with native-born Americans, or even other immigrants, a common definition of upward mobility and the good life. Consequently, immigrant behavior in the marketplace was often misunderstood.

Chapter Four treats in detail that pressure to assimilate which every immigrant encountered soon after arrival. There were numerous economic and social incentives for the immigrant who would abandon his culture and adopt the language and customs of his new home. Well aware of what was at stake, the members of each group tried to choose carefully which aspects of American life they would embrace and which they would resist. This chapter also discusses the role of public schools, political parties, and settlement houses as institutional vehicles for the transformation of aliens into proper Americans.

Chapter Five examines immigrant response to nativism, the fervent opposition to immigration. The new immigrants were confronted with both ad hoc and highly organized crusades directed against them by native Americans bewildered and threatened by the strange customs and sheer number of the newcomers. This chapter traces the gradual spread of anti-immigrant sentiment, which culminated in national laws restricting immigration, latching shut the golden door.

Finally, a brief conclusion looks to the impact of the immigration experience on both the travelers themselves and the society they entered. When the costs of introducing twenty-three and a half million strangers into America were tallied, how were those costs shared? Ultimately, was it worth the price of leaving family and friends, shucking old habits and beliefs, to become an American?

This book does not pretend to be either a comprehensive or an exhaustive study of the immigrant experience from 1880 to 1921. The very size and diversity of the new immigration would make a single-volume study a Sisyphean task. But it is that very diversity which this book hopes to indicate. The "huddled masses" exist only until the morning mist blows clear to reveal individuals and families standing separately and resolutely. On closer examination, the faces of this "wretched refuse" take on a determined, rather pugnacious expression. The immigrant experience was neither romantic nor glamorous; many people starved, many retreated into taverns or insanity. But the great number of new immigrants made a success of their lives, mapping out goals according to their own specifications, making those compromises with American society which they considered necessary. And in the end, the *contadini* of the *Mezzogiorno,* the bearded Jews of the *shtetlach,* the burly peasants of the Steppes, and the French Canadians of Quebec changed America even as they were changed by it.

ONE

Emigration: A Matter of Change and Choice

The "new immigration" which made its debut in the United States between 1880 and 1921 was but one act of a much larger production. During this period, millions of individuals in various regions of the globe decided to leave their homes, some permanently, but many others only temporarily. While migration has always been part of human history, at no other time did people go so far, so quickly, so cheaply. The telegraph, the railroad, and the steamship allowed emigrants to learn of conditions abroad, travel less expensively, arrive more quickly and safely than previously, and, if they chose, go home again. Between 1887 and 1888 alone, it is estimated that a million people left the continent of Europe for destinations in the United States, Canada, Australia, New Zealand, Argentina, Uruguay, and Brazil. Countless others remained in Europe, but migrated from their towns or villages, usually to larger towns and cities, frequently to those in western Europe. In their wake, these restless people shattered not only their own economic and social patterns, but those of the communities they left and joined.

Most often, emigrants ventured abroad deliberately, not in a spontaneous somnambulism occasioned by traumatic upheavals. They were not drawn from their homes against their wills, as if by a "distant magnet." Emigration was but one among various choices; not even the most popular in every region of southern and eastern Europe and Asia. After all, the vast majority of the people in these places never left their communities. And not all who left were struck with "American fever," as it was called, though this country did receive the largest share of newcomers throughout the period.

Emigrants from Italy, Austria-Hungary, the Balkans, and Russia were also sailing toward Canada, Argentina, and Brazil. At the same time Australia, was receiving immigrants from southeastern Europe and Asia. The mighty wave of immigration was breaking upon many beaches. Moreover, neither the United States nor the other nations receiving immigrants at this time were disinterested observers of the moving millions. Economic competition born of industrialization stimulated a spirited race among industrializing nations to lure within their borders vast quantities of cheap, unskilled labor.

I

Countries in western Europe and the Americas competed for emigrants from eastern regions of Europe and part of Asia between 1880 and 1921. And as their labor supply gradually drained westward, unwilling donor nations launched their own counteroffensives in the propaganda war to stop the flow. In 1887, local officials in Austria were instructed by the Ministry of the Interior to oppose foreign efforts to recruit their country's labor force. That same year, the Greek Minister of the Interior ordered local officials to publicize the hardships of trans-Atlantic ocean voyages. In 1905, the provincial government of Croatia-Slavonia published dire warnings about the gravity of economic conditions in the Americas. Aside from persuasion, most countries did not interfere with emigration, hoping only that it would be temporary. Migratory laborers often relieved the pressures of poverty and unemployment in their home country, finding jobs elsewhere and sending money back to their families. Emigration was thus a kind of safety valve that relieved the threat of domestic unrest in countries under economic stress. Greece, Italy, Hungary, Japan, and Mexico, among others, welcomed home seasonal workers who returned from abroad regularly with their earnings. It is estimated that between 1897 and 1902, 500 million lire or almost $100 million entered Italy in the pockets of returning emigrants, who quickly circulated their capital in their country's economy by purchasing real estate, building homes, or opening small businesses. Emigration, then, was often as beneficial to the economies of donor nations as it was to those of the receiving nations.

By 1900, the Canadian government was spending over $1 million annually to lure foreign labor. Most of the funds were used to maintain offices in sixteen cities in the United States. Agents were given a commission of $300 a head to persuade the recently landed emigrants to continue their journey the relatively short distance to the Canadian border. Offices in London distributed the *Canadian Settlers Handbook* which provided glamorous descriptions of wages, job opportunities, prices, and immigrant living conditions. Ironically, even as the Canadians advertised for European workers, French Canadians were crossing the border in pursuit of higher wages in America's mills and factories.

The Brazilian government, badly in need of labor after the

abolition of slavery in the 1880s, sought to establish agricultural colonies of immigrants. The Brazilians offered to provide immigrants with trans-Atlantic and inland fares, permit duty-free entry of personal belongings, grant full civil rights to all new arrivals, and repatriate widows, orphans, or disabled workers at minimal charge.

Argentina was extremely aggressive in the recruitment process and was the United States' closest competitor for immigrants in the late nineteenth century. Though immigrants were required to pay their own ocean fares, they were guaranteed by the Argentinian government several days free lodging after arrival and free inland travel. Agents assisted the immigrants in purchasing land or finding employment in agriculture. Books describing Argentina, often profusely illustrated, were distributed at European ports.

The United States government, in contrast to Argentina and Brazil, did not offer subsidized fares, immediate naturalization, or any other direct inducement for the enlistment of immigrants. While it offered the same open-door policy to immigrants as did the other countries, recruitment was conducted by agents employed by private companies in need of workers or by steamship lines anxious to fill their vessels to capacity. The popularity of the United States as a destination for emigrants was the product of a fortuitous combination of economic opportunity, political liberty, and religious tolerance.

As it had from its earliest days, the United States offered newcomers an unusually high degree of economic opportunity. During the early and mid-nineteenth century, much of that opportunity involved land ownership. The United States possessed a vast domain and had a tradition of land distribution based upon the fee-simple pattern rather than a feudal or semi-feudal system. This meant land could be purchased or sold or rented for money or its equivalent in goods without incurring further obligations beyond taxes. The federal government assumed a limited role in land distribution, its primary concern being the development of equitable procedures for distributing land to private citizens who would settle on it and contribute their labor to its improvement.

In 1862, Congress passed the Homestead Act to induce settlers to migrate beyond the Mississippi. This Act provided that the head of a household could acquire a quarter section of land consisting of 160 acres, settle it, cultivate it for only five years, and then acquire legal title to that land. Only citizens of the United States were eligible, or those who had formally declared their intention to become citizens. However, impoverished immigrants such as those crossing the Mexican border often lacked the capital to finance settlement of even public lands. Speculators and railroad companies were quick to purchase huge tracts of land to resell later at inflated prices. Those immigrants lucky enough to have some money were often gouged as they naively accepted mortgages at interest rates as high as 60 percent.

Still, there were opportunities for newcomers who insisted upon working the soil. As Andrew Rolle discovered in his study of the Italians in rural America (*The Immigrant Upraised,* 1968), the vineyards in California required the labor of thousands of agricultural workers. Opportunities for truck farming existed in New Jersey and New York's rural counties, and small farms in New England, barely larger than gardens, were available. Southern Italians who wished to grow fruits and vegetables for sale could thus become commercial farmers on a small scale.

By the 1880s most immigrants found that cities offered them more plentiful economic opportunities than the countryside. The United States was beginning a period of rapid industrial expansion which necessitated a ready supply of cheap, unskilled, and semiskilled labor for factories and mines. Thus, the industrial sector of the American economy generated jobs that were increasingly claimed by workers from abroad. In the New England states, the Irish and British immigrants of an earlier era competed for jobs with newer French Canadian arrivals. By 1910, a study of twenty-one industries reported that 52.9 percent of all employees were foreign-born, some two-thirds of them from the countries of southern and eastern Europe. In some industries such as textiles, clothing manufacturing, ore mining, meat-packing, slaughtering, and cigar manufacturing, the percentage was far higher. Like the Irish who landed in the 1840s, Slavs, Poles, and Italians frequently found jobs in railroad and construction work, two areas traditionally dominated by foreign-born labor.

The hours were long and the wages low, but compared to the immigrants' native countries, the United States seemed rich in opportunity for the dedicated. Those who wanted work found jobs. And the apparent fluidity of the economy and social structure gave hope to those who yearned to be self-employed. Some Irish and German immigrants of an earlier era had opened small businesses of their own, or had seen their children become entrepreneurs. Their modest successes encouraged newcomers in the belief that America was the portal to independence and security—perhaps even wealth.

By the end of the nineteenth century the United States already held a worldwide reputation as a haven for the victims of political oppression and religious persecution. Individual liberties were guaranteed by a written Constitution and Bill of Rights. Because of the country's federal system and the vast size of the nation, the national government and its agents hardly touched the lives of most individual Americans during the nineteenth century. Rarely did federal laws place minorities at a legal or political disadvantage. However, state and municipal laws often codified local prejudices. For instance, Sabbatarian laws barred Jews from doing business on Sundays and Catholic parents were required to pay public school taxes to discourage them from paying additional tuition to parochial schools. A 1906 law in San Francisco segregated the mere handful of Japanese children into separate schools.

State laws were relatively minor inconveniences compared with the legal restrictions on land ownership, university enrollment, and physical mobility suffered by some immigrants in their homelands. East European Jews, who arrived in droves after the turn of the century, appreciated especially the absence of officially sanctioned anti-Semitic policies. Religious liberties were protected by the Constitution, and the orthodox among the east European Jews discovered that if they lived in America they would be able to worship publicly without fear of government reprisals or systematic persecution.

This favorable and attractive report of the United States

reached those contemplating emigration by three distinct routes: newspaper articles, printed publicity disseminated by private companies, and letters sent to relatives and friends from those who had already made the journey.

Though literacy was not universal in southern and eastern Europe, where most new immigrants originated, every community had some inhabitants who could read their native language. Newspapers were expensive, but often an educated individual—a doctor, a merchant, a teacher—subscribed or several townsmen shared a subscription. Sixty years after his arrival in the United States, a Russian immigrant interviewed by the Smithsonian Institution in Washington, D.C., recalled the sharing of a Yiddish newspaper published in Moscow after its arrival in his native rural village. When the weekly newspaper arrived at the post office, the recipient was expected to read the headlines aloud to all who gathered within earshot. This spate of news usually stimulated discussion and debate, so trips to the post office were never quick errands. In the case of joint subscriptions, each subscriber took a turn keeping the paper for a few days. While retaining the paper, each subscriber might also invite neighbors home for another reading and more discussion. The newspapers often had articles about the United States, and, thus, life in America became a matter of interest in the post offices and homes of these small Russian communities.

To each village that "lost" some members to the New World, letters arrived describing travails and triumphs. The names of far off places—New York, Chicago, Brooklyn, Philadelphia—mentioned in newspaper articles took on a new meaning when former neighbors and relatives lived there. In her memoir, Mary Antin (*From Plotzk to Boston*, 1899) recalled that in Russia, "America was in everybody's mouth. Businessmen talked of it over their accounts; the market women made up their quarrels that they might discuss it from stall to stall; people who had relatives in the famous land went around reading their letters for the enlightenment of less fortunate folk. . . . children played at emigrating; old folks shook their sage heads over the evening fire and prophesied no good for those who braved the terrors of the sea and the foreign goal beyond it; all talked of it, but scarcely anyone knew one true fact about this magic land.'' Whatever the anxieties and distresses of life in America, immigrants in their letters usually minimized the obstacles confronting them, preferring instead to report in extravagant detail all that was good in their new environment.

This image of the exaggerated bountifulness of America detailed in immigrant letters was skillfully reflected in pamphlets and posters published by private companies, railroads, and steamship lines. Material printed for mass distribution was designed to sell land, ocean passages, or seats on American trains. Agents, some from America, others hired on commission to represent American companies to their countrymen, dispersed these publications in foreign ports, in towns and villages. In the first half of the nineteenth century, such books and pamphlets about America were circulated throughout northern and western Europe, especially in England and the German states. Because many Americans considered northern and western Europeans to be more desirable settlers than southern and eastern Europeans, advertising continued to be directed at the former area late in the nineteenth century, despite the apparent shift in migration patterns. In 1891, Thomas Cook and other British agencies were still distributing folders describing the virtues of Chicago, Milwaukee, and St. Paul in northern and western European cities, though the flow of immigrants was originating in other parts of Europe.

Though information in these pamphlets was often outdated, they continued to be widely circulated. New immigrants departing for America from western European ports read about opportunities that no longer existed. For example, by the turn of the century, there was little land still being distributed by railroad companies in the American west at prices immigrants could afford. Yet, the Thomas Cook agent in Antwerp still distributed the company's pamphlet ''Homesteads For All'' with its assurances of abundant low cost land.

Trans-Atlantic steamship lines also advertised and competed vigorously for passengers. The port cities in Germany and England, from which many of the new immigrants departed, buzzed with agents seeking customers. In the southern provinces of Italy, one hundred and sixty agents pursued the traveling trade, with four thousand subagents who were often village shopkeepers or tradesmen. Some of the guidebooks issued by steamship companies focused on the size and stability of the vessels or the comfort of the accommodations. Others stressed the speed of the journey or the low cost.

Steamship company pamphlets contributed to immigrants' distorted image of America, occasionally including poems or American success stories to encourage those who might waver at the pier. Colorful posters of America's scenic beauty covered the walls of Greek coffee houses and grocers' shops. No doubt, the same was true in other parts of southern and eastern Europe. These inspiring poems and posters portrayed a world that would prove elusive to newly arrived immigrants.

The counterbalance of fact and fantasy that moved those who departed for the United States can never be calculated. The United States did offer unparalleled economic possibilities and guarantees of individual liberty. However, there can be little doubt that intolerable economic and social conditions at home were critical catalysts in precipitating migration. It may well be that glowing letters and ebullient propaganda were more influential in determining where the emigrants would go rather than whether or not they would go at all. Pamphlets may have prompted the choice of New York or Chicago over Rio de Janeiro or Toronto, but it is unlikely that even the most embellished description could budge a family basically content with its lot. The stereotype of an immigrant dreaming of "streets paved with gold" is, nevertheless, a reminder of the persuasive power of fantasy. The colorful posters and exuberant letters, if not completely truthful, unquestionably made the future seem ever sweeter and emigration to the United States especially tantalizing to those bent on moving.

II

Who actually emigrated to America in the years between 1880 and 1921? Until the turn of the century, most were young males in their teens or early adulthood, who had left their parents or young wives and children behind as they pursued opportunity abroad. Immigration officials estimated that 78 percent of the Italian and 95 percent of the Greek immigrants were men. Asian emigrants in the period also tended to be young males. However, after 1900, the character of migration changed among some groups. By 1920, 48 percent of southern Italian arrivals were female. Among Poles, the proportion of men to women was almost evenly divided. And among Slovaks, female immigrants outnumbered males 65 percent to 35 percent. In other groups, however, the newcomers continued to be mostly male. Almost 80 percent of the Greek arrivals were men and boys in 1920.

American immigration officers often referred to these young male immigrants as "birds of passage," because they followed a regular pattern of migration to and from the United States. In the period between 1908 and 1914, U.S. immigration officials recorded 6,709,357 arrivals and 2,063,767 departures. During this period, more than half of the Hungarians, Italians, Croatians, and Slovenes returned to Europe. From 1908 through 1916, 1,215,998 Italians alone left America. Statistics indicate that only 67 percent of all immigrants settled in the U.S. However, the figures are suspect because federal authorities did not systematically monitor departures. It may be that many fewer individuals than originally estimated actually emigrated because some of the same individuals were counted as new arrivals each time they reentered the country after an absence. Generally, though, repatriation averaged a fairly steady 20 to 30 percent of immigration with annual and seasonal variations.

Italian, Greek, and Slavic men in particular ventured forth in the spring, remained abroad until late fall, and returned home for the winter months. Seasonal patterns of migration were especially common for outdoor laborers in agriculture, mining, or construction and were affected by the availability of jobs. Those who could not find work or had been unable to save sufficient earnings to return paid the penalty of remaining in the United States during the bleak winter months. Canadian workers took advantage of the open border to migrate back and forth at will. In the Southwest, Mexican laborers with visas, and often those without, arrived for planting and harvesting seasons, returning to Mexico when jobs were scarce.

Annual variations were the products of economic fluctuations, changing conditions in home countries, and domestic American policies. An Immigration Commission report on migration patterns for 1907–1908 explains: "The fiscal year 1906–07 being one of unusual industrial activity, was marked by the largest immigration in the history of the country, but following the beginning of the industrial depression in October of the fiscal year 1907–08 there was a sudden reversal of tide, and during the remainder of that year there was a greater exodus. . . ." As World War I loomed over Europe, record numbers of people seeking to avoid hostilities fled to America, bringing 2,400,000 newcomers in 1913–1914. Others, fearing separation from family by wartime restrictions, streamed home, the volume of repatriation rising from approximately 200,000 in 1910 to 300,000 the following year and remaining high for the next three years. After the war, labor strikes and economic depression in the United States, and a general distrust of foreigners and supposed radicals combined to enlarge the number of returnees to 660,000 between 1919 and 1921.

But many who planned to return home to live never did so. Constantine Panunzio, an Italian immigrant described in his recollections (*The Soul of an Immigrant*, 1921) how too little money and a series of small, personal crises delayed by twelve years his return to Italy. By that time he had become a naturalized American and no longer wished to return home for longer than a visit.

The east European Jews were the exception to the rule. In 1908, the peak year of Jewish immigration to the United States, only 2 percent returned to Europe according to available data. Comparative estimates of returnees during the entire 1880–1921 period range from a high of nearly 90 percent for Balkan males to a low of 5 percent for east European Jews. Few of the Jewish emigrants were "birds of passage." Those who made the journey to America usually brought their families, suggesting that most came to settle rather than to reap a quick profit and return.

Jews, often fleeing religious persecution as well as pursuing economic advantages, hoped to find in the United States a haven from oppression.

Other European minorities chose to embark for the United States for similar reasons. Members of ethnic minorities, especially, did not feel bound to the lands of their birth. Germans living in Slavic countries, Greeks residing in Romania, Croats and Serbs in Hungary, Turks in Bulgaria, and the French in Canada, among others, often felt the sting of discrimination and sometimes were the target of official and unofficial acts of repression. There was little hesitation to leave and seek a permanent residence elsewhere when the opportunity arose.

Whatever their pattern of migration or their plans for the future, most immigrants arriving in the United States were leaving from southern and eastern Europe, not northern and western Europe as they had in earlier years. In his 1912 study, *The New Immigration,* Peter Roberts defined the immigrants as "people emigrating to America from the countries of southeastern Europe." Along with many others, Roberts had noticed that southeastern Europeans had begun to appear in the "immigration stream in the early eighties of the last century." He was also aware that the flow had become a torrent, and that by 1896, these new immigrants accounted for almost 80 percent of all new arrivals. The chart on pages 20–21 demonstrates the shift from northern Europe to Austria-Hungary, the Russian Empire, Italy, and the smaller countries of Romania, Turkey, and Greece.

Approximately 4,500,000 Italians entered the United States between 1880 and 1921. Over 80 percent of them came from *Il Mezzogiorno,* the southern provinces of Italy. The total migration out of Italy changed its course and intensity several times during this period. Until the late 1880s, most of Italy's annual migration, approximately 100,000, left for the Western European countries to the north. As more Italians chose to emigrate—300,000 after 1895 and 500,000 in most years after 1900—more chose to go farther than Europe and cross the Atlantic. Before the turn of the century, the most popular desti-

DECENNIAL IMMIGRATION TO THE UNITED STATES, 1880–1919

	1880–89	Percentage	1890–99	Percentage	1900–1909	Percentage	1910–1919	Percentage
TOTAL	5,248,568		3,694,294		8,202,388		6,347,380	
Northwestern Europe								
United Kingdom[1]	810,900	15.5	328,759	8.9	469,578	5.7	371,878	5.8
Ireland	674,061	12.8	405,710	11.0	344,940	4.2	166,445	2.6
Scandinavia[2]	671,783	12.7	390,729	10.5	488,208	5.9	238,275	3.8
France	48,193	0.9	35,616	1.0	67,735	0.4	60,335	1.0
German Empire	1,445,181	27.5	579,072	15.7	328,722	4.0	174,227	2.7
Other[3]	152,604	2.9	86,011	2.3	112,433	1.4	101,478	1.6
Central Europe								
Poland	42,910	0.8	107,793	2.9	not returned separately		not returned separately	
Austria-Hungary	314,787	6.0	534,059	14.5	2,001,376	24.4	1,154,727	18.2
Other[4]	—	—	52	[6]	34,651	0.4	27,180	0.4
Eastern Europe								
Russia[5]	182,698	3.5	450,101	12.7	1,501,301	18.3	1,106,998	17.4
Romania	5,842	0.1	6,808	0.2	57,322	0.7	13,566	0.2
Turkey in Europe	1,380	[6]	3,547	0.1	61,856	0.8	71,149	1.1
Southern Europe								
Greece	1,807	[6]	12,732	0.3	145,402	1.8	198,108	3.1
Italy	267,660	5.1	603,761	16.3	1,930,475	23.5	1,229,916	19.4
Spain	3,995	0.1	9,189	0.2	24,818	0.3	53,262	0.8
Portugal	15,186	0.3	25,874	0.7	65,154	0.8	82,489	1.3

Other Europe	1,070	(6)	145	(6)	454	(6)	6,527	0.1
Asia								
Turkey in Asia	1,098	(6)	23,963	0.6	66,143	0.8	89,568	1.4
Other	68,673	1.3	33,775	0.9	171,837	2.1	109,019	1.7
America								
British North America[8]	492,865[7]	9.4	3,098[7]	0.1	123,650	1.5	708,715	11.2
Mexico	2,405[7]	(6)	734[7]	(6)	31,188	0.4	185,334	2.9
West Indies[9]	27,323	0.5	31,480	0.9	100,960	1.2	120,860	1.9
Central and South America	2,233	(6)	2,038	0.1	22,011	0.3	55,630	0.9
Other Countries								
Australia[10]	7,271	0.1	3,225	0.1	11,191	0.1	11,280	0.2
Other	6,643	0.1	16,023	0.4	40,943	0.5	10,414	0.2
		100.0[11]		100.0		100.0		100.0

[1] England, Scotland, Wales
[2] Norway, Sweden, Denmark
[3] Netherlands, Belgium, Switzerland
[4] Bulgaria, Serbia, Montenegro
[5] Includes Finland and boundaries prior to 1919
[6] less than one-tenth of one percent

[7] Immigrants from British North America and Mexico not reported from 1886 to 1893
[8] including Canada
[9] including Jamaica
[10] including Tasmania and New Zealand
[11] Totals are rounded to nearest percent as in Census report.

From N. Carpenter, "Immigrants and Their Children," U.S. *Bureau of the Census Monograph*, No. 7 (Washington, D.C., 1927) pp. 324–25.

nation was Latin America, especially Brazil. In 1897, 104,510 Italians emigrated to Brazil, while only 59,431 came to the United States. However, just a year later the trend began to reverse, and two years later in 1900, fewer than 20,000 Italians landed in Brazil, while over 100,000 disembarked in the United States. Argentina also surpassed Brazil and moved into second place in the competition for cheap labor from Italy. Though some Italians still would not migrate beyond western Europe, an ever-inceasing number of emigrants chose a country in the Americas. Economic opportunities were more plentiful across the Atlantic, and improved transportation brought America closer to Italy for "birds of passage" who preferred to spend the winter with family and friends.

Some countries, such as Russia, experienced losses primarily among minority elements of the population. In 1907, Russia lost 250,000 people to other countries. Of these, 115,000 were Jews and 73,000 were Poles (approximately 4 percent and 6 percent of the Russian population, respectively). Most of the others were Lithuanians, Finns, and Germans. Though 66.8 percent of the country's population were of Russian ethnic stock, only a tiny fraction of that group emigrated.

It is impossible to know precisely to what degree non-Russian emigrants left Russia for economic rather than political reasons. However, for one group—the Jews—the attraction of western Europe and the Americas was the freedom from the violent religious persecution, or pogroms, they suffered at the hands of bloodthirsty mobs. In Russia and Poland, pogroms against the Jews were conducted by Christian mobs with the consent and often the cooperation of local police and civil leaders. Three waves of pogroms occurred in Russia, each more destructive than the last: 1881–1884, 1903–1906, and 1917–1921. Although violent persecution had all but disappeared in western Europe by the end of the nineteenth century, pogroms persisted in Russia and elsewhere in eastern Europe.

The United States already had a reputation for religious freedom, though many Jews feared that a liberal, secular democracy inspired by the Reformation and the Enlightenment would prove a difficult climate in which to sustain orthodoxy. Therefore, the orthodox, the better educated, and the relatively prosperous tended to remain behind. Between 1880 and 1900, most of the 1,000,000 Jews arriving in the United States were young, relatively uneducated, and anxious to improve their lot. However, after 1900, a gradually increasing number of intellectuals and prominent businessmen were lured to America from Russia as well as Romania and other easten European countries by the prospect of escape from escalating persecution, byproducts both of famine and political discord. Ninety-one Jewish teachers arrived in 1895, as compared with the 269 who came to America in 1907; 197 "other professionals" landed in 1891, 1,045 in 1907. After 1905 many members of the Jewish socialist movement, or Bund, came, some to avoid jail, others discouraged with the minimal possibilities for change in eastern Europe.

Even as the "new immigrants" from southern and eastern Europe were crowding America's ports, immigrants were raining down upon the United States from the north. Since the mid-nineteenth century, French Canadians had crossed the open border with the United States to work in mines, mills, quarries, and lumberyards. Most were farmers from Quebec forced to find work elsewhere because of the depressed state of agriculture in French Canada. Outmoded agrarian methods had depleted the soil, and what little land there was available for new farms was often inaccessible to markets because of inadequate roads and bridges. In addition, the old French inheritance system prevailed. Holdings already too small were further subdivided among the many offspring of French Canada's large families, reducing farms to strips too narrow to yield an adequate living.

When upper and lower Canada were joined in 1840, the Dominion of Canada's government made every effort to encourage immigration from Europe because French Canadians refused to settle the extensive lands of western Canada. Instead, the French Canadians became itinerant workers in America, intending to return with the money they saved to rebuild family farms and pay off debts. While some laborers found work in northern New York, western Pennsylvania, and Ohio, the majority headed for nearby New England, where they competed with Irish laborers who had replaced the Yankee farm girls in textile factories. Over 40,000 French Canadians fought for the Union army during the Civil War, many just to collect the bounties.

In the late nineteenth century, Canadian emigration to the United States increased and many of those who came remained to take advantage of opportunities in New England's burgeoning industrial economy. French Canadian immigrants were a ready source of cheap, industrious, and uncomplaining labor. New England Yankees dubbed them "the Chinese of the Eastern States," regarding them as poor, ignorant, degraded, and resistant to Americanization. The immigrants' Catholicism fueled Protestant Yankee antagonisms. Nevertheless, railroads continued to transport French Canadians across the border, while Canadian officials tried futilely to stop the emigration with legislative investigations, ecclesiastical admonitions, and propagandistic literature which imputed to the emigrants such base motives as extravagance, love of luxury, and adventurism.

In the period from 1890 to 1900, the number of Canadian-born French immigrants in the U.S. increased by over 90,000. In 1896, a wave of Canadian prosperity and the election of the first French Canadian Prime Minister deterred many French Canadians from leaving and brought others home. Yet, by 1900 there were more than 500,000 French Canadians in New England. Between 1900 and 1910, the French Canadian immigration began to decline, but only 10 percent ever returned permanently to Canada.

As French Canadians filtered into the industrial economy in the northeastern states, Mexican immigrants penetrated the southwest's agrarian economy. When the treaty of Guadalupe Hidalgo ended the Mexican War in 1848, approximately 75,000 Mexicans lived in the Southwest, with the largest concentrations in the regions which became California and New Mexico. However, economic development in the southwest at the turn of the century brought Mexican laborers across the border in droves. Whether they came legally or illegally, permanently or temporarily, for the day or until the planting and harvesting cycle was completed, Mexican laborers were plentiful and worked cheaply. They helped complete southwestern railroad lines; made southern California, Texas, and Arizona into cotton country; and dug irrigation ditches that turned California's Imperial and San Joaquin valleys into a fertile cornucopia. Mexicans mined in Arizona, harvested fruit in Texas and California, and staffed packing plants all over the Pacific coast.

Impoverished Mexican migrant laborers crossed the border easily and often, taking jobs once held by Asian laborers. Crowded by a sharply increasing population and propelled by economic and political turmoil, Mexican workers migrated northward, often risking the penalties of illegal entry. But during World War I, all contract labor laws were suspended for the war's duration and thousands of Mexicans who could not previously obtain visas were welcomed by growers to cultivate the crops needed for the war effort. Mexican immigrants were welcome whenever there was a labor shortage, but they were not welcome as permanent residents striving for citizenship.

Economic dislocation brought thousands of Asian immigrants to the United States between 1880 and 1921. Most of the Chinese who emigrated to the United States were impoverished agricultural laborers from Toishan, a district of Kwangtung in southern China. Unable to survive as farmers, some Toishanese turned to commerce and left for the States from the port of Hong Kong. By 1880, the number of Chinese in the United States was still only about 100,000, concentrated mostly on the west coast. Nativists and west coast laborers who feared economic competition from this cheap labor supply fought for the passage of the Chinese Exclusion Act in 1882. This Act virtually halted emigration from China to the United States until after World War II.

The largest Asian group to arrive in the United States during the late nineteenth century was the Japanese. However, early emigrants did not go to the United States, but to Hawaii, then a sovereign nation. In 1868, 148 Japanese contract laborers went to Hawaii. Many were unhappy with their decision and were returned by the Japanese government to their homeland. During the next seventeen years, Japan did not permit any contract laborers to leave the country.

As the worldwide demand increased, the Hawaiian economy became progressively dependent upon a single crop, sugar cane. Cheap plantation labor became crucial, and the Japanese were a ready supply of willing laborers. Economic turmoil in Japan, including severe inflation, unemployment, and subsequent social unrest left the Japanese government searching for a safety valve. Hawaii was the answer. In 1885, an agreement between Hawaii and Japan brought twenty-six ships carrying 28,691 Japanese to Hawaii between 1886 and 1894. The Japanese who answered the call for contract labor came primarily from the prefectures of Hiroshima and Yamaguchi. Over 300 people in the first group of 600 to depart for Hawaii came from one spot on one small island, Oshima District on Yamaguchi.

Because farming and fishing alone could not support Oshima's dense population, islanders often took second jobs as carpenters or stone cutters and other trades for supplemental income. Their wives engaged in home industries such as weaving cotton. Then, in 1884 economic pressures were worsened by a typhoon and landslide. Two years later, the emigration began. Not everyone who applied to leave Oshima was accepted. Married couples were given preference. However, by far the greatest number of applicants were single men, 40 percent of whom returned to their villages in Japan after their contracts expired. They usually returned with sufficient funds to pay their debts, buy small plots of land, or build homes.

Emigrants from Hiroshima Bay followed a slightly different pattern. Seven hundred and seventy-seven migrated over a fifteen year period—624 to Hawaii, 151 to the United States, and small groups to Canada, the French West Indies, Peru, and Australia. All but 10 of the 194 females in the group were married. Emigration from this area affected the moderately well-off as well as the needy, but many of those who left returned to Japan. One village later became known as "American Village" because, of its 1,687 inhabitants, one-sixth had been born in

Canada or the United States during the period of migration, and seven of the village's ten families still had relatives abroad. Still, most did not return even to that village. Fifty-one families had emigrated permanently in the earlier period, taking everyone along.

In general, most Japanese emigrants to Hawaii were young agricultural laborers or small peasant-farmers. Males left more frequently than females by a ratio of four to one. The poorest left first, followed by those who were better off but still in search of better economic opportunities. Those Japanese who went to Hawaii were unskilled laborers, while those who traveled to America generally came from more prosperous districts and higher social classes than those who contracted to work on the sugar plantations of Hawaii. Of those who sailed for America most were merchants, students, and skilled laborers.

The "new immigrants" did not pour forth equally from every corner of the globe or from every rank of society. Dramatic shifts in world migration patterns between 1880 and 1921 brought an increasing number of southern and eastern Europeans westward, Chinese and Japanese eastward, Canadians southward, and Mexicans northward. The trans-Atlantic migration increased sharply, first to Latin America and to Canada, and later primarily to the United States. The migrants most frequently intended their stay to be temporary, and for some it was, but for millions more, the umbilical cord that tied them to their birthplaces was irreparably severed. Most of those in motion were from society's poor, and many oppressed as well. In the first decades of the migration, males were in the vanguard but, from at least some groups, married and single women soon swelled the exodus. Officials at the most popular destinations such as the United States scrambled to keep count of the travelers. However, statistical compilations only revealed who was coming and where they were coming from. Beyond the numbers lay the explanation as to why this mass of humanity was in motion and why the discrete human beings involved chose to undertake the journey.

III

It is platitudinous to characterize a particular historical era as "a time of change." Every period in human history includes transformation—great or small. The economic and social alterations of nineteenth-century Europe were not unprecedented intrusions into stagnant societal waters. What created a crisis of vast proportions were the changes in how people lived. The family, the church, the social hierarchy, the political establishment—the cement of community in traditional European societies—proved unable to absorb the shock waves of change. A rapidly increasing population, the decline of an aging agrarian system, and the emergence of the industrial revolution fractured traditional political, economic, and social relationships. And when people lost confidence that long respected political institutions and social customs could stabilize their lives, they sought to cope with their anxieties not collectively, but as individuals making decisions for their own personal welfare.

Migration had always been an option for populations plagued by the ravages of starvation, disease, or conquest. Now, technological advances made emigration an even easier, safer, and cheaper choice than it had been before. And so, in southern and eastern Europe, many individuals packed their belongings and left—if only temporarily—to escape these disruptions beyond their control.

For southern Italians, the most unsettling change was a sharp upsurge in population. As early as the 1870's, the natural increase per year was slightly over 6 per thousand, as compared with 3 per thousand several decades earlier. By the 1880's, the figure had risen to 11 per thousand. Meanwhile, Italian mortality figures fell from 30 persons per thousand annually to under 20 per thousand in the years from 1870 to 1910. Only halfway through the forty-year period did birthrates show a marked decline. Despite the major Italian emigration that proceeded throughout the period, the total population of the country actually rose by more than 6,000,000 persons between 1880 and

1910. In 1895 alone, births exceeded deaths by some 350,000. Similar figures available for Poland and other parts of eastern Europe, while not quite as dramatic, confirm the increase in population for the continent.

The greater the number of people, the greater the competition for the resources of life, especially economic resources. Agriculture was the foundation of the economy in southern and eastern Europe. While rural populations of countries in the west were decreasing in size by 1850, the rural population of eastern Europe did not level off until well into the twentieth century. As the general population increased, there was a decrease in the size of family farms.

Landlords took advantage of inheritance laws to displace newly emancipated peasants and divide estates into small plots of land for rental at high prices. In Bulgaria, fewer than 4 percent of all holdings exceeded 50 acres, while over 100,000 farms appear to have been less than 2½ acres in size. Often plots composing a farmer's holdings were scattered geographically. In Galicia, in 1900, only about fifteen hundred holdings exceeded fifty acres, half a million were 7½ to 50 acres, while six hundred thousand were between 2½ to 7½ acres. More than two hundred thousand holdings were even smaller.

Some European peasants manufactured small articles in their homes during the long winters. The products of such cottage industries were marketed locally and regionally. In Poland and the Slovak countries, women kept looms and flax in their homes with which to make hats, linens, lace, and rugs, while their husbands and sons carved objects from wood to be sold at market. Individuals owning a mule often performed local services, hauling wood or stones for neighbors, or engaging in long-distance transport of goods over the plains of Galicia or the western provinces of Russia as had their fathers and grandfathers before them.

Industrialization disrupted the traditional economic structure of southern and eastern European nations, transforming habits of work and altering avenues of commerce. Mechanization in agricultural areas, such as the wheat fields of Hungary, reduced the need for migrant labor. The railroads, which had once provided construction work for laborers throughout the eastern half of the continent, were now completed, making obsolete the services of those whose hands had built it. No longer would goods be hauled overland by mule, nor would there be as many ships involved in the coastal trade. Railroads were faster and cheaper, but, inevitably, provided fewer jobs for those at the bottom of the socioeconomic scale. Railroads linked areas of manufacturing, bringing goods to even remote regions more cheaply than those same items could be produced by cottage industries.

As economic opportunities shriveled in rural provinces, they increased in cities. Urbanization, the helpmate of industrialization, upset traditional life-styles that had remained unchanged for centuries. Farmers, artisans, and unskilled laborers in rural communities experienced economic uncertainty and many migrated to cities to work in the factories, machine shops, mills, and distilleries. Austria's urban population trebled between 1843 and 1900. From 1850 to 1900, Vienna's population sprang from 431,000 to almost 2,000,000. Warsaw quadrupled in population during the same half century. While the populations of easten European countries remained essentially rural, the trend was clear and migration quickened. Large towns burgeoned; large cities grew to metropolises.

Entrenched governments of countries in southern and eastern Europe brought little relief to their people. These nations had long been characterized by wide discrepancies between the very rich and the very poor. Wealthy landowners and merchants exercised control over the state and saw little reason to initiate any social or economic reforms. Industrialization frequently shifted power from landowners to a new middle class, but social change was limited. Labor strikes, such as those in Italy and Hungary in the 1890s, precipitated only minor reforms, and the Romanian peasant revolt of 1907 failed to accomplish any major improvement. The autocratic governments of southern and eastern Europe, aware that economic and technological influences beyond their control were transfiguring their countries, sought to resist, for as long as possible, any adjustments that would shift the balance of power. Taxes were kept high and bulging urban areas made it easier than ever to impose compulsory military service. The political climate became increasingly repressive.

For millions of politically hamstrung southern and eastern Europeans, then, emigration appeared to be a path to relief from the pressures of overpopulation, agricultural change, and industrialization.

Modernization cast its confusing mantle over all regions, lending a thread of similarity to the stories of widely diverse ethnic groups. Case studies of the southern Italians and east European Jews can illuminate the specific pressures that caused substantial numbers of these groups to emigrate in the late nineteenth and early twentieth centuries. Separate geographically, and disparate culturally, these groups are, nevertheless, worthy of comparison because both were threatened by overwhelming transformations in lifestyle. Substantial numbers of both groups emigrated, preferring the risks that leaving entailed to the uncertainties in store for those who remained behind.

All of the provinces of the newly unified Italian nation were affected in some way by the country's expanding population, changing agrarian order, and increasing industrial production during the last two decades of the nineteenth century and the first two of the twentieth. However, the drastic effect of this upheaval on the country's southern provinces coupled with a long history of poverty in that part of Italy made many southern Italian farm laborers, or *contadini,* especially willing to risk a long journey and separation from their beloved *paese* ("village") if only temporarily.

Those who have studied the Italian-American experience, such as Joseph Lopreato (*Italian Americans,* 1970) and Richard Gambino (*Blood of My Blood,* 1974), have emphasized the connotations of Il Mezzogiorno, which means "the land that time forgot." Governments came and went, but the Mezzogiorno remained the same. For the contadini, *la famiglia* ("the family") and *l'ordine della famiglia* ("the rules of family behavior and responsibility"), not the government determined how one lived.

Long and bitter experience with government officials and the large landholders they protected left the contadini with a cynical attitude toward all forms of authority other than the family. The cynicism summed up by the adage *la legge va contrai cristiani* (the law works against people) was not dispelled by the unification. The lot of the contadini deteriorated; reform never filtered south.

The northern Italians who controlled the new government were largely unconcerned about the south. Those who thought of the region at all considered it populated by lazy, impoverished, irresponsible, crude, and often violent primitives, rather than shrewd, hard-working, independence-loving, family-oriented contadini. The results were legal and economic impositions that strangled the Mezzogiorno. The tax burden on the south was increased considerably, and the region was trapped in a maze of increasing debt. In Sicily alone, the tax rate increased 30 percent over the rate imposed by Bourbon monarchs before unification. The large landowners, the *latifondisti,* quickly established an understanding with the government similar to that which they always had and evaded the new tax burdens. While cows and horses, most often the property of the wealthier latifondisti, were exempted from taxation, mules and donkeys, the mainstays of the contadini, were taxed heavily. Church lands, confiscated by the new government, were almost always transferred to the latifondisti, almost none being distibuted to the contadini.

In Italy, tenants were more common than actual owners. Some southern Italians were sharecroppers, with the landlord providing the capital and renewing the tenancy from generation to generation, thus perpetuating an almost peasant-like attachment to the land among tenants. Other tenants had to provide their own working capital and renew their tenancy at frequent periods. There were also combinations of different arrangements. Some peasant farmers owned part of the land they cultivated, but rented other plots. Landlords, too, played varied agricultural roles. The same landowner could be an active manager on one of his estates and an absentee landlord, dependent on a hired manager, on another estate. There were also large estates that resembled antebellum plantations in the American South. These were cultivated by large gangs of poorly paid laborers, who hoped to one day own even the smallest plot of land.

Tax burdens imposed upon them forced the contadini to mortgage their lands and take loans, often from agents of the landowners. Interest rates ranged from 400 percent to 1000 percent. Inexorably, landlords captured land through defaults; a report to the Italian Parliament in 1910 stated that several hundred latifondisti owned or controlled over 50 percent of the land in the Mezzogiorno. According to Leonard Covello (*The Social Background of the Italian-American School Child,* 1944), in Calabria there were 121 landowners per thousand inhabitants in 1882, but only 91 per thousand by 1901. In Sicily, the reduction was from 114 to 94 per thousand, between 1882 and 1901.

Not all southern Italians farmed. Some were artisans, and worked in factories manufacturing textiles such as silk. To protect northern industry, high tariffs were passed by the central government. These crippled the unprotected industries of the Mezzogiorno and unemployment rose markedly. The agony of the Mezzogiorno was intensified in the last third of the nineteenth century by a series of natural disasters. The vineyards, the nucleus of the southern Italian economy, were devastated by a blight, phylloxera, which had originated in southern France. The disease, coupled with heavy French tariffs on Italian wines and competition in the world market by American citrus products from Florida and California, crushed the economy of certain provinces. Calabria, Apulia, and Sicily, known for their wines, were hardest hit. The competition of oranges and lemons from the United States also stifled the citrus industry in Basilicata, Calabria, and Sicily.

In 1905, a series of earthquakes jarred Basilicata and Calabria. In 1906, another natural disaster occurred when Vesuvius erupted, burying a whole town near Naples in the province of Campania. Etna erupted in 1910. However, the worst disaster, by far, was the earthquake and tidal wave that struck the Strait of Messina between Sicily and the Italian mainland in 1908. The city of Messina was leveled and over 100,000 of its inhabitants killed. Over three hundred smaller towns were destroyed. In the city of Reggio di Calabria alone, another 20,000 died. Natural disasters such as these were rarely the root causes of emigration, but often they were catalysts.

The Jews of eastern Europe had historically been an oppressed minority. The people of the diaspora first began to migrate eastward in the thirteenth century when Boleslav the Pious, King of Poland, opened his kingdom to settlement by European Jews. The monarch hoped the Jews would function as money lenders, tax collectors, merchants, innkeepers, and artisans, fostering prosperity in his backward agrarian nation. Because of their crucial role in Poland's economy, Jews were protected by the law and a growing number of western European Jews settled there.

Despite periodic episodes of persecution such as the Chmielnicki massacres between 1648 and 1655, Jewish civilization survived and at times even prospered until Poland was conquered and divided in the eighteenth century. The majority of Poland's Jews fell under Russian rule, while the rest lived in areas controlled by Austria and Prussia. The tsarist government viewed the Jews through a prism of superstitious apprehension, despising them with medieval fervor as Jesus' betrayers and fearing the enlightened minds and affluence of the Jewish middle class. To undermine Jewish influence, the government sought to divert Jews from commerce into agriculture and confined most of them to the Pale of Settlement. The Pale was an area of about 386,000 square miles from the Baltic Sea to the Black Sea. It included Congress, Poland, Lithuania, Byelorussia, and the Ukraine (excluding Kiev). A few Jewish merchants managed to survive in the cities and even prosper, but most Jews found themselves in the Pale, attempting either to farm the desolate steppes or scratch a living as artisans and craftsmen in small towns.

Life in the Pale fluctuated between periods of repression and periods of toleration. The reign of Tsar Nicholas I, 1825–

1855, had been a period of Jewish suffering. In addition to periodic expulsions from villages, there was interference in the cultural and religious life of the Jewish community. Books printed in Yiddish and Hebrew were heavily censored, the curriculum of Jewish schools was "adjusted" by government officials. Worst of all, perhaps, were the conscription laws that commandeered boys—especially those of the poorer classes—between the ages of twelve and eighteen for periods of military service up to twenty-five years. Because of the economic restrictions against them, Jews were especially vulnerable to conscription. Jewish parents, too poor to bribe officials, often either hid their sons or assisted them to flee.

Tsar Alexander II was politically moderate, and under his rule the Jews had a much easier time. By 1874, military service was reduced to six years. A small number of Jews were permitted to enter the universities, and Jewish businessmen were allowed to travel to parts of Russia from which they had been excluded. Even so, most Jews continued to live in rural poverty.

Many of the traditional roles played by Jews in the Russian economy were altered when Tsar Alexander II freed the serfs in 1863. Jews had worked as middlemen, selling the produce raised on feudal estates by the peasants or functioning as nobles' agents in distant cities. With emancipation, the nobles took more direct control of their affairs and eliminated the expense of middlemen. Jewish merchants in small towns and cities became economically expendable. Only a few fortunate merchants rose to economic prominence in Moscow, St. Petersburg, or Kiev.

By the 1880s Russian tyranny hardened. Laws were passed prohibiting Jews from owning or renting land outside towns or cities and discouraging them from living in villages. Jewish students, subjected to harsh quota systems, were frequently excluded from secondary schools and universities. Jewish merchants who had remained in the cities were now expelled without warning. By 1897, over four and a half million Jews lived in the Pale, 94 percent of Russia's total Jewish population.

Most Jews in the Pale lived marginal existences in villages or *shtetlach*. One observer described a *shtetl* as a small town with cobble streets and "a jumble of wooden houses clustered higgledy-piggledy about a market place . . . as crowded as a slum. . . . " (Maurice Samuel, *The World of Sholom Aleichem,* 1943). The streets were winding, turning into alleys and lanes, and reemerging, all in no particular pattern or design. The center of the town was always a marketplace, "with its shops, booths, tables, stands, butcher's blocks." Every day, except during the winter, peasants from the surrounding area brought their livestock, produce, fish, hides, and grains to market. In exchange, they purchased from Jewish merchants a selection of hats, shoes, dry goods, boots, lamps, oil, and other manufactured products. Jews bought and sold, and bargained with customers, conducting business only yards from their homes. Legal restrictions placed on their residences and occupations by the Russians hobbled the Jewish community economically. According to renowned Jewish historian Salo Baron,

In many communities, fully 50 percent of the Jewish population depended on charity. . . . In Russia, as in other countries going through the early stages of modern capitalism, the rich grew richer, while the poor became more and more indigent. . . . It has been estimated that in many communities up to 40 percent of the entire Jewish population consisted of families of so-called luftmenschen, that is, persons without any particular skills, capital, or specific occupations.

Jews with skills and those without them strangled on Russian restrictions. It is little wonder, then, that even before the political turmoil and pogroms at the end of the nineteenth century, some of the poorest Jews had begun to migrate westward. Many were able to go only as far as Germany or England before their funds were exhausted. Of this group, some found jobs and settled in western Europe, while others stayed only briefly to earn enough for the next leg of the journey to America.

Unable to own land, displaced from their homes and villages as a matter of government policy, the Jews, unlike the southern Italians, had little affiliation to the land on which they lived or to the larger community that oppressed them. The Jews' heritage was based upon a history and religion that defined and codified appropriate behavior. Their religion and its traditions shaped the pattern of the east European Jews' existence and sustained them. As Irving Howe (*The World of Our Fathers,* 1976), described it, "The world of the east European Jews was a world in which God was a living force, a Presence more than a name or a desire. . . ." Jews had an intimate relationship with their God, praying to Him in Hebrew but speaking to Him in Yiddish, the mixture of Middle High German, Hebrew, and Russian that was the colloquial language of the Pale. To survive culturally, as well as physically, Jews disciplined their life with religious ritual. There were ritual commandments to cover almost every aspect of life, from the marriage ceremony to how the shoes should be put on each day. Life on the *shtetl* was strengthened by religious observance, but it was a narrow, rigid life.

In the early nineteenth century, these demanding protective religious ideas were challenged by liberal thought from the countries of western Europe. Just as the ideas of Voltaire, modified by two centuries and filtered through western Europe, were affecting the thoughts of Russian intellectuals, this *Haskala* or Enlightenment captured the hearts and minds of many Russian Jews, especially the young. Fresh ideas—individualism, liberty, socialism, Zionism—and a craving for social and economic change challenged the credibility of the rabbinate and fragmented Jewish communities.

The assassination of the relatively liberal Tsar Alexander II in 1881 by a group of nihilists who had been living in the home of a Jewish woman had severe repercussions for the Jews. The subsequent harsher program of Tsar Alexander III and the brush fire of violence that swept through Jewish communities in the aftermath of the assassination caused many Jews to flee their homes. Some left Russia, journeying to western Europe and the United States. Others began the move to large cities within the Pale in their struggle for survival.

Younger Jews often moved from the *shtetls* to the slums of Minsk, Vilna, Warsaw, and Bialystok in search of work. They were at the mercy of employers and often worked fourteen to sixteen hours a day for wages as low as two or three rubles per week. They organized to improve conditions and, in the last two decades of the nineteenth century, a socialist labor party, the Jewish Labor Bund, led strikes that improved conditions, if only temporarily.

The economic turmoil was compounded by new violence. The escalation of religious persecution, especially the bloody Kishinev massacre of 1903 in which forty-nine people were killed and more than five hundred injured, persuaded many remaining Jews to finally leave Russia. Those already gone now sent for wives, children, and parents.

There were thus two phases to Jewish emigration from Russia. Between 1880 and 1900, Jewish immigrants tended to be those displaced merchants and impoverished artisans of the Pale in search of economic opportunity. After the turn of the century, however, the increasing intensity of pogroms and other forms of religious persecution encouraged rabbis, secular intellectuals, the wealthy, and middle-class businessmen to depart as well. Young Jewish socialists disheartened by an abortive revolution in 1905 also packed up their dreams and headed westward. The east European Jewish immigration swelled only as other options were exhausted.

Neither the southern Italians nor the east European Jews were strangers to hard times. However, in earlier periods people had coped with crises by turning to the values and institutional structures of their group. Southern Italians found in their families sanctuary from the oppression of landowners and government officials. East European Jews drew sustenance from ancient traditions to ward off the indignities of discrimination and the pain of persecution. Few members of either group ever migrated far from family and community, though individuals occasionally left the country for the town to find work. However, the unprecedented pressures of modernization in the late nineteenth century combined with advances in transportation and communication to make long distance migration a viable option. Individuals could emigrate across borders on railroads and across oceans on steamship at a cost affordable to nearly all. News of conditions abroad could be more accurately and quickly transmitted. More information and faster, cheaper modes of travel turned emigration into an escape hatch for large numbers of people, rather than the isolated, adventurous individual.

The experiences of the southern Italians and Russian Jews exemplify those of other new immigrant groups. For all new immigrants, emigration from their homelands was only one of many options and usually not the first considered. Most preferred to remain in their native countries and familiar communities as long as possible. Those barred from certain occupations learned others. Those removed from the land moved to the cities; others moved to different regions in their country or crossed the border into an adjoining country. Most remained where they were, expecting to earn enough money to survive and hoping that circumstances might change so their children would enjoy the prosperity that eluded them. But many refused to wait and deliberately chose emigration. Even among the emigrants, however, there were those "birds of passage" who regarded their departures as temporary. Home governments reconciled themselves to the migratory patterns beyond their control. A Hungarian law in 1881 provided that emigrants would be permitted to leave the country only on authorized shipping lines. For nearly a quarter of a century, no line was so authorized. However, when this and other measures failed to stop the exodus, the Hungarian government consoled itself with the license fees collected from transportation companies by the Ministry of the Interior. Similar legal impediments by other countries also foundered and were removed.

Those individuals who left were often attracted by the blandishments of advertising, especially the stories, poems, and songs that exalted life in the United States and the other countries of North and South America. Others read the same literature and still preferred to stay at home. In the final analysis, the emigration of particular persons was idiosyncratic; some were more adventurous than others. Always, though, the emigrants had options other than leaving. Departure was rarely other than a deliberate choice.

Were there regrets among the immigrants at leaving their cities, villages, regions or counties? Some believed that whatever they found abroad would be an improvement over what they were certain to suffer at home. One former resident of County Komarom in Hungary wrote home from America:

Here a man is paid for his labors and I am certainly not sorry that I am here. I work from six in the morning until seven at night and get $10–11 a week.... There are 10,000 workers in this shop and my wife is working here too. She makes $9.50 a week. At home I made that much money in a whole month and people thought my job was very good. Here I am sewing dresses on a machine. In America there is no difference between one man and another. If you're a millionaire you are called a Mister just the same, and your wife is Missis.

Dr. George M. Price no doubt expressed the feelings of many east European Jews—and probably many non-Jews—when he considered whether or not he regretted emigrating from Russia. His diary reveals his conclusion:

Sympathy for Russia? How ironical it sounds! Am I not despised? Am I not urged to leave? Do I not hear the word zhid (Jew) constantly? Can I even think that some consider me a human being capable of thinking and feeling like others? Do I not rise daily with the fear lest the hungry mob attack me? ... It is impossible ... that a Jew should regret leaving Russia.

Constantine Panunzio, in contrast, retained warm memories of Italy and felt himself bound to it by "wonderful, inexplicable tendrils which so intertwine themselves around our human hearts in our infancy as to make the country of our birth, the very village, or hamlet in which we first saw the light of day, the one spot on earth around which cluster the sweetest of life's memories."

Whether they looked back with nostalgia or with rancor, most new immigrants who arrived in the United States elected to stay. Many wrote letters or made return visits in order to coax relatives and friends to join them. Apparently, their efforts were successful; 92 percent of the people arriving at the port of New

York between 1908 and 1910 declared that they were joining friends or relatives who had sent for them.

The migration of millions from the Old World to the New was symptomatic of the requirements and side effects of modernization in both places. Ironically, even as modernization propelled people out of their homes, upsetting their communities and abolishing their livelihoods, it eased the ordeal of travel through technological innovation. Still, even when external events encouraged exodus, the ultimate decision to pack up and go remained with the immigrants themselves. It was a gamble; no one could possibly foresee all the ramifications of setting off across continents and oceans. But it was a gamble chosen deliberately and often chosen with hope and enthusiasm.

T W O

The Journey and the Reception

The emigrant leaving his community, that "man at the cross-roads," as described by Oscar Handlin in *The Uprooted,* "moved alone." Though social and economic metamorphoses had affected his neighbors no less than himself, uprooting entire towns and villages, emigration was an individual act. Most of his neighbors would never leave; the emigrant stood alone at life's intersection or with only his family by his side. The knowledge that others were making similar decisions could at best have been only moderately comforting.

The emigrants' ordeal began almost as soon as the decision was made to pack. In addition to the emotional strain of leaving, they faced weeks of travel, hardship, and expense, with the distinct possibility that they might fail to reach their destination. Still, the emigrants were never completely at the mercy of people and processes beyond their control. Individual immigrants often exercised their cunning to detemine whether craft or cash was the best lever for prying loose required certificates and passports from recalcitrant officials. Nor should it be forgotten that even the humblest travelers were consumers, their patronage prized by competing railroad and steamship lines. Those reaching America would be examined and questioned by immigration officers who would judge whether they were sufficiently physically fit, mentally able, and morally sound to merit passage through the "golden door." Here the immigrants relied upon their guile and hints gleaned from the letters of earlier arrivals to help them vault the final hurdle.

Clearing the threshold did not end the ordeal, however. In the weeks and months ahead, the new immigrants would face the task of finding the necessities of life—shelter, food, and a job— even as they adjusted to the strange ways of the New World. In America resourcefulness and persistence would be the staunchest allies.

For most, the city would be their decompression chamber. Job opportunities and scant knowledge of the country beyond the streetlights kept most new immigrants huddled together in the growing urban centers of the Northeast and the Midwest. There newcomers would sink their roots through cracked pavement and begin the final stage of the odyssey, the transformation from aliens to Americans.

I

Once the decision to leave was made, emigrants began the process of uprooting themselves psychologically as well as physically. Fears and anxieties had to be overcome, friends and relatives bid painful farewell, and belongings sorted through for departure. The distance to America seemed vast and the journey so laced with danger that at times parents and children parted fearing they would never see each other again. Often they were correct.

In the tiny communities of southern and eastern Europe, where the fate of each affected all, the news of an emigration occasioned public reaction. In her memoir (*The Promised Land,* 1912), Mary Antin recalls the day she received the steamer ticket sent by her father in America: "Before sunset the news was all over Plotzk. . . . Then they began to come. Friends and foes, distant relatives and new acquaintances, young and old, wise and foolish, debtors and creditors, and mere neighbors—from every quarter of the city. . . . a steady stream of them poured into our street, both day and night, till the hour of our departure." On the day of departure, a procession of townspeople escorted the family to the train station, Antin recalls:

The procession resembled both a funeral and a triumph. The women wept over us, reminding us eloquently of the perils of the sea, of the bewilderment of a foreign land, of the torments of homesickness that would await us. They bewailed my mother's lot, who had to tear herself away from blood relations to go among strangers; who had to face gendarmes, ticket agents, and sailors, unprotected by a masculine escort; who had to care for four young children in the confusion of travel, and very likely feed them trefah [non-kosher food] or see them starve on the way. Or they praised her for a brave pilgrim, and expressed confidence in her ability to cope with gendarmes and ticket agents, and blessed her with every other word, and all but carried her in their arms.

Leaving for America was a triumph, but one tinged with regret and the loss of a part of one's life and identity.

The emotional trauma of departure was compounded by the physical trials of the trip to the New World. First came the trek over land to the port of embarkation. For Italians and Slavs, the problem was largely logistical; how to cover the hundreds of miles that might separate one's village from the ocean. Many hiked for days and weeks, their belongings on their backs and in handcarts they pushed or pulled. Those who could afford it came in horse-drawn wagons they owned or rented. By the turn of the century, the European railway system was so complete that the journey to port was neither exhausting nor risky for most travelers. Special trains, often subsidized by the steamship companies, brought emigrants to the coast. German ports were used by approximately two-thirds of the emigrants from Austria-Hungary, though some did wander all across Europe to Liverpool, England, before leaving. After 1900, Austria and Hungary tried to secure within their borders the profits from the profitable business of shipping emigrants, and their carriers competed with the English. In 1904, the Hungarian government signed an agreement with the Cunard Line, headquartered in Liverpool, to begin sailing from its port of Fiume to New York under the name of the Cunard Hungarian American Line. The line held the monopoly on transporting America-bound immigrants and, in return, agreed to abide by Hungarian emigration laws, accept only Hungarian official documents, and place Cunard agents only at ports designated by the Budapest government. The agreement backfired when competing shipping lines lowered their rates drastically and immigrants proved willing to cross Hungarian borders illegally and sail from other ports for rates as low as eight dollars. The competition and Cunard's overcrowded ships resulted in not more than a third and sometimes as little as one-fifth of Hungarian travelers departing from Fiume.

East European Jews had to cope with special hazards in addition to the high cost and inconvenience of travel suffered by all emigrants. In *World Of Our Fathers,* Irving Howe explains that Jews often traveled by indirect routes to port cities in western Europe to circumvent the anti-Semitic policies of some east European nations. Many Russian emigrants found ocean passage from Odessa longer and costlier than a railroad trip across Europe and a voyage from a north European port. However, most Jews took care to cross the Russian border into Austria-Hungary instead of Romania on their way west because "the Romanian authorities were feared as particularly savage anti-Semites, while the Austro-Hungarian empire seemed mildly benevolent.'' Because Russian port officials often used passport inspection as an occasion for harrassing Jewish males old enough for military conscription, Jewish immigrants in the north refused to purchase the expensive Russian passport, and, instead risked an illegal border crossing into Germany. Many Russian Jews arrived in America bearing tales of their daring escapes across the border, aided by a paid agent and bribes. In his ''Memoirs of a Russian Immigrant,'' (*American Jewish Historical Quarterly,* LXIII, September 1973), Max Vanger described his adventure:

...we went by wagon to a place not far from the Prussian border, where we stayed in a granary. We were forbidden to talk or smoke, and we would hear the Russian cossacks riding on their horses. We stayed in that building until dark, and someone came to us and told us to come along. Whatever luggage we had was taken from us. We rode in a wagon until we reached a wooden section. In a short time there was a large group, perhaps fifty people and a leader. He told us not to talk to one another, not to smoke or light a match, and if we heard someone nearing us to lie down on the ground. It was dark and needless to say all of us were scared, but nothing happened. Finally we were told to stop walking. We did and the agent went ahead of us. He was gone awhile and came back and told us to walk in a single line which we did and after a short distance, two soldiers facing one another with rifles on their shoulders counted us. We were told that this was the border between Russia and Prussia, and the soldiers received one ruble a head for letting us through.

Once across the border, the emigrants rode by train to their port of departure in western Europe.

Following an especially virulent wave of anti-Semitic violence in Romania in 1899, small groups of Jews left the country on foot. These *fusgeyers* (''wayfarers'') hiked hundreds of miles, living off the land and the charity of sympathetic peasants along the route to the sea. Fusgeyers often pledged to share with their fellows their last morsel of food. According to Irving Howe, fusgeyers tramped through the countryside singing songs in Yiddish and sometimes even offered amateur shows in villages along the way to raise funds. However, such romantic episodes were rare. More frequently, Jews sought to remain anonymous, hoping to cross the border into Austria or Germany without incident.

Jews were not alone in suffering inconvenience and exploitation. All emigrants were vulnerable. Hungarian emigrants departing Fiume were required to secure birth certificates and present them to government officials prior to departure. Male emigrants were checked for liability to military service before passports were issued. Since only those in possession of passports could buy tickets, bribery and the sale of falsified papers was quite common. All emigrants also had to undergo a medical examination before leaving, the result of increasingly stringent American health standards for immigrants. By 1907, nearly 40,000 people were rejected by physicians at European docks. At busy ports such as Liverpool, Havre, Trieste, Fiume, and Palermo, American physicians or those selected by American consuls worked with local doctors representing steamship companies or European governments. However, no procedure proved perfect and medical certificates, like passports, were often available even to the ineligible for the right price.

Philip Taylor in *The Distant Magnet* (1971) and Maldwyn Allen Jones in *Destination America* (1976) offer lengthy descriptions of emigrant processing procedures. At Naples, the ship lines issued ration-tickets and travelers were sent to a licensed hotel and then to a restaurant for dinner, which often consisted of a thick soup or stew, melon, and wine. Vendors along the way peddled all manner of food to those still hungry. On the day the ship was scheduled to depart, American consular officials saw each emigrant and provided vaccinations. After a final medical inspection by an American doctor and a last check of papers, the emigrants boarded and made last minute purchases of food, tobacco, and lucky charms from merchants in small boats bobbing around the anchored ship.

At Liverpool and western European ports, the steamship companies vied with each other to make the transfer from train to ship as smooth and comfortable as possible. Company employees met trains and transported emigrants to lodgings inspected and regulated by the companies. Such preparations shielded the travelers from thieves and confidence men. The Cunard Line built a complex of buildings that could house 2,000 people at a time in ten-bed dormitories with good sanitation and food. Kosher food was available for Jewish emigrants and staff members could speak a variety of east European languages. Perhaps the most elaborate facilities were built by the Hamburg-Amerika Line. The Line constructed an immigrant village for transients with its own railway station, churches, and a synagogue. Travelers could bathe while their clothes and luggage were disinfected. The emigrants were then examined by doctors and provided with inexpensive lodgings and food.

Though the facilities were an improvement over the neglect of the early nineteenth century, the inspection routine seemed dehumanizing. Emigrants resented being poked, jabbed, washed, and sprayed. However, shipping lines insisted upon the procedure to curtail shipboard illness and avoid the expense of returning emigrants to Europe who had been refused admission to the United States by American inspectors.

During the cholera panic of 1893, in Rotterdam, the routine became even more elaborate. While their clothes were being disinfected, travelers were ordered to take an antiseptic bath. Males received close haircuts after a shampoo with a mixture of soft soap, carbolic acid, creolin, and petroleum that was applied with a stiff brush. Women and girls did not receive haircuts, but did receive shampoos and were required to use fine tooth combs to remove lice from their hair. The process was undignified, but after 1891, American immigration law required that the steamship companies vaccinate, disinfect, and examine their immigrant passengers prior to sailing; that they reimburse the United States government for the housing of detained passengers at American ports; and that they return rejected immigrants back to their ports of embarkation free of charge. Most immigrants complained but preferred the inconvenience to being turned away.

By the 1890s, the trans-Atlantic journey took less time and was safer than it had been earlier in the century, before the age of steam. The potential dangers of such a trip, such as fires, shipwrecks, and collisions, were reduced by the ship inspection conducted by European governments and the advent of iron ships. However, it was still an uncomfortable voyage for immigrants, most of whom traveled in steerage. Steerage referred to the one or more below-deck compartments of a ship located fore and aft where the ship's steering equipment had been located in an earlier era. The steerage compartments of late nineteenth-century steamers were no more than cargo holds without portholes and only two ventilators per compartment, unpartitioned, and six to eight feet high, crammed with two or more tiers of narrow metal bunks. Travelers had to bring their own straw mattresses which were cast overboard on the last day of the voyage. Men and women were segregated, sometimes on separate decks but often by nothing more than some blankets draped over a line in the center of the compartment. Children were permitted to stay with their mothers. Some of the larger ships sailing the Atlantic crammed as many as 2,000 men, women, and children into compartments unfit for any human habitation.

The threat of steerage epidemics was reduced by the shorter number of days spent at sea, an average voyage taking between eight and fourteen days. Yet, there were still occasional epidemics of typhus and smallpox on board ship. The air was always fetid because of the poor ventilation. Emigrants had to bring their own cups, plates, and utensils. They cooked their own meals in one of several small galleys shared by all those in steerage. In the galleys were ranges, boilers, and a few vegetable cookers. Many immigrants brought food with them. However, most had to buy at least some of their provisions on board ship. They paid high prices, and the fare provided was almost always the same—herring. The ship companies provided herring because it was inexpensive, nourishing, and helped to combat sea-sickness. Toilet facilities varied from vessel to vessel. Some earlier ships had as few as twenty-one toilets per thousand emigrants. Later vessels had one toilet for every forty-seven travelers.

The details of the journey's hardships suggest that even

before they reached America, the immigrants began a readjustment in their lives. They learned to live in close proximity to those from different countries who practiced different customs and who worshipped God in different ways than they did. Many began the slow and painful process of compromising some of their own values and customs to the demands of the environment. And finally, most newcomers in steerage mastered the art of survival under the severe stresses and strains of daily life in a strange environment, far from the support of family and friends. Immigrants were weaning themselves from the Old World even before they landed in the New.

However, not all the compromises were made by the travelers. As consumers, immigrants patronized steamship lines, which competed for their lucrative trade by improving shipboard conditions. A popular innovation was the elimination of steerage travel. After the turn of the century, ship companies built third-class accommodations in new ships. Third-class facilities were considerably less sumptuous than the first two classes but far more comfortable than steerage accommodations. All emigrants were in two-, four-, and six-birth cabins. There were more toilets and washrooms, a small covered promenade, and even lounges and smoking rooms. Meals were served in small dining areas and kosher food was provided. Bars sold beer, soft drinks, and tobacco. Ship lines provided an increased number of nurses and physicians, and after a papal statement in 1906, many ships provided chaplains to serve the spiritual needs of passengers.

The news that land was in sight triggered enormous excitement in the weary emigrants on board. Despite the orders of the captain and the crew's efforts, newcomers pushed close to the rails on deck. Children were lifted high above the crowd. Nighttime dockings postponed the thrill until morning. Those who arrived at the port of New York gazed in awe at the tall buildings on shore. Filled with anticipation, and some apprehension, everyone scrambled to wash and to dress in their best clothing. There was often much anxious speculation as to what questions American customs officials and immigration inspectors might ask. Immigrants who had made the journey before coached the novices at the last moment on what to say and what not to say.

The dock was chaotic. Passengers were separated by class to collect their baggage. Orders were shouted in various languages, officials raising their voices over the shouts of vendors selling fruit and other refreshments to the bewildered travelers. The immigrants had arrived in America, but the journey was not over yet. A ferry boat waited to transfer all passengers to a depot where they would be inspected, examined, questioned, processed, and either admitted or rejected. The majority would be admitted and permitted to embark upon the next stage of their journey.

The new immigrants fortunate enough to get close to the ship's rail might have tried to catch glimpses of their future, even as they prepared to discuss their past with immigration officers. As they stumbled down the gangplank, their legs may have been shaky and their heads light from the physical rigors of the voyage, though the trip had been safer, faster, and cheaper than an earlier wave of immigrants to the United States had experienced. As they stepped on dry land, they may have crossed themselves or murmured a prayer. Perhaps they thought about all they had left behind even as they rushed to board the ferry for what lay ahead.

II

In the years prior to 1850, the admitting of newly arrived immigrants into the United States was casual, and records were kept haphazardly by local port officials, when they were kept at all. However, the deluge of 4,500,000 immigrants from northern and western Europe by mid-century persuaded state officials at major ports to adopt more systematic procedures and to provide specific facilities for receiving the newcomers.

Between 1855 and 1892, after docking in New York, the busiest port of entry, the immigrants would have been taken by ferry boat to Castle Garden at the tip of Manhattan Island. The

Garden had been built as a fortress shortly before the War of 1812, only to be converted into an amusement center and concert hall. In 1850, Jenny Lind, the Swedish Nightingale, made her American debut there. Five years later, the chaos created by hundreds of thousands of immigrants forced the State of New York to begin operation of the Garden as America's first Emigrant Landing Port. Other states with major ports such as Massachusetts, Maryland, and Pennsylvania also haphazardly tried to cope with the problem.

The overwhelming new emigration from southern and eastern Europe placed an increasing strain upon what few American immigration facilities there were. Responding to reports of abuses and inefficiency, Congress appointed the Ford Committee, to investigate state immigration procedures. The Committee's report in 1889 was highly critical of the states' ability to cope with the magnitude and character of the new immigration. And the report reflects an important change in the attitude of American officials toward the immigrant. Earlier in the nineteenth century, state officials had been primarily concerned with protecting the immigrant against the hardships of America. Now state concern shifted to protecting America from potentially dangerous elements in the immigrant population. One witness testified that because of its inability to weed out undesirables among the large numbers of seemingly impoverished arrivals, New York State spent $20 million annually in care for paupers and the insane. A federal law in 1891 established a Bureau of Immigration to curb such inefficiency and to regularize immigration procedures. The Bureau assumed the responsibility of protecting America from those it defined as unfit to care for themselves and, therefore, likely to become public charges. Inspection of all newcomers was designed to effectively bar "idiots, insane persons, paupers or persons likely to become public charges, persons suffering from a loathsome or dangerous contagious disease, persons who have been convicted of a felony or other infamous crime or misdemeanor involving moral turpitude, polygamists, and also [those] assisted by others to come, unless it is affirmatively and satifactorily shown on special inquiry that such person does not belong to one of the foregoing excluded classes, or to the class of contract laborers. . . ."

Later legislation sharpened the criteria for exclusion. A 1903 law made specific mention of beggars, the insane, prostitutes, and anarchists as unfit for admission. Four years later, Congress again expanded the categories of unacceptable aliens to include the feebleminded, imbeciles, persons with physical or mental defects which might affect their ability to support themselves, those afflicted with tuberculosis, children under 16 unaccompanied by their parents or legal guardians, and persons who admitted to have committed a crime of moral turpitude or engaged in prostitution. It also raised the penalty against shipping companies carrying immigants found to be unfit by U.S. officials. A comprehensive law enacted in 1917 included all the categories of the earlier laws and added some new classes for exclusion. One new provision required all immigrants to be able to read and write a language. The literacy requirement was especially aimed at the peasants of southern and eastern Europe. It was a thinly veiled attempt to discriminate against the new immigrants.

New federal guidelines called for extensive and careful examination of each immigrant seeking admission, a process that included mental and physical tests. The federal government ordered procedures in all American ports standardized and new facilities provided, where necessary, to handle the task. However, most ports continued to process immigrants in a casual fashion. All passengers traveling first or second class were exempt from any inspection or careful scrutiny. In Boston, Philadelphia, and Baltimore doctors and inspectors rushed through procedures on board ship or in a small shed on shore. New York City was different. Because New York was by far the most popular port of arrival, Congress abandoned Castle Garden for a new and larger immigration depot on Ellis Island in 1890.

A low-lying islet, close to the New Jersey shore, Ellis Island was doubled in size with landfill. Armaments stored there since the Civil War were removed. An initial wooden structure was built to receive immigrants but it burned in 1897. The following year the federal government ordered the construction of an enormous complex of red brick buildings to house the immigrant processing depot. It was completed in 1901. The first floor of the main building held baggage handling facilities, railroad ticket offices, food sales counters, and a waiting room for those traveling beyond New York. A mezzanine floor held observation areas and, later, administrative offices. The registry room or Great Hall on the second floor was the largest room, 200 feet long, 100 feet wide, and 56 feet high. The floor space was divided into narrow alleys by iron railings. Also on the second floor were detention areas, offices, waiting areas, and special inspection offices.

The iron railings more than any other physical characteristic of Ellis Island intimidated many immigrants. The bars were erected only to create aisles to facilitate orderly movement, but newcomers saw them as the iron bars of a prison. Detention areas, separated from the rest of the floor by wires, were perceived as cages by frightened immigrants.

Ellis Island became the model for all inspection depots. Five thousand immigrants per day could be handled easily and often many more were rushed through inspection. Nearby, another building housed a restaurant, laundry, and shower facilities capable of bathing 8,000 people per day. There was a powerhouse and, across the ferry slip, a man-made island with a new hospital. The eating facilities and food especially are remembered by those who entered through Ellis Island. Long after her journey to America, one woman remembered her amazement at the dining room's appearance. "There were long tables and benches, and everything was on the table, fish, vegetables, whatever, water, water pitchers. These people, they really looked pathetic, most of them, but they seemed to enjoy their food. . . ." The food itself was alternately described by newcomers as tasty and terrible, as interesting and as institutional rot. Often the fare aroused curiosity and awe: "I never saw a banana in my life," recalled one Slavic woman, "and they served a banana. I was just looking at it." Others who ate it with the skin on soon learned how to peel it.

Although the time spent at the island depot was usually only a few hours, the experience was, for many immigrants, the most traumatic part of their voyage to America. Contemporary American journalists such as Broughton Brandenburg, who investigated the system on Ellis Island, were impressed with its thoroughness and "the kindly, efficient manner in which the law was enforced." Some writers conceded, however, that the immigrants had to contend with language problems, fears, and insecurities that no investigative reporter could fully appreciate. Professor Edward Steiner, who had himself emigrated to the United States, cautioned, "Let no one believe that landing on the shores of 'The land of the free and the home of the brave' is a pleasant experience; it is a hard, harsh fact surrounded by the grinding machinery of the law, which sifts, picks, and chooses, admitting the fit and excluding the weak and helpless." Thomas Pitkin, in *Keepers of The Gate* (1975), suggests that immigration officials were defensive about the austere appearance and coldly efficient operation of Ellis Island, denying its reputation as "a cross between Devil's Island and Alcatraz." The experience that led some immigrants to refer to Ellis Island as the "Isle of Tears" or "Heartbreak Island" can best be appreciated by following a single immigrant through the gruelling inspection procedure.

After arriving on Ellis Island, the immigrant was approached by a uniformed officer who pinned an identity tag on his clothing. The tag was inscribed with an identification number, corresponding to that in the ship's manifest. As he climbed the stairs to the main hall, carrying all his luggage, the immigrant was quite unaware that the first test had begun. "Line inspection" took place at the top of the stairs and was designed to permit physicians to scrutinize the immigrant under conditions of physical stress such as that produced by carrying heavy luggage up a flight of stairs. Hands, eyes, and throats were closely examined. The heart of an immigrant who had carried his luggage up the stairs could be easily judged strong or weak, and the exertion would reveal deformities and defective posture.

The immigrant was given a stamped identification card to hold in his hand. As he examined the card, he was observed by physicians to check for defective eyesight. His eyelids might then be checked for trachoma. This painful examination involved the use of a glove buttonhook to turn the immigrant's eyelids inside out. His scalp was probed for lice. He was also required to turn his head so that his facial expression could be examined. Certain expressions were believed by the examiners to be indicative of mental disorders.

As he proceeded to the great hall, the immigrant might have noticed that others leaving the examination area had chalk marks on the right shoulders of their garments. Letters marked in chalk stood for the particular disability which might cause that immigrant's detention, or even rejection: L for lameness, K for hernia, G for goitre, X for mental illness, and so on. All who failed to pass the medical exam were detained for a more thorough inspection. Sometimes a few days of rest and some nourishing food was sufficient to prepare an immigrant for reexamination.

An immigrant fortunate enough to pass this first series of tests was now herded into one of the pipe-railed alleyways that led to the immigration inspectors. With the help of interpreters, the inspectors would ask each immigrant a series of questions. What is your name? What nationality? Marital status? Occupation? Who paid the passage? Is that person in the United States? How much money do you have with you? Have you ever been in a prison or an almshouse? After 1917, all immigrants were required to demonstrate literacy in a language. Often the inspector, who did not speak a foreign language, gave the immigrant a card with an instruction written in his native tongue, such as "Scratch your right ear." Immigrants who did so were presumed to have read the card and to be literate.

Names were a source of puzzlement for the immigration inspectors. Not all immigrants could spell their names in English, and perplexed inspectors often recorded names as they sounded or occasionally took the liberty of shortening or "Americanizing" a name. Millions of Americans still bear these "Ellis Island" names. The story of Sean Ferguson, apocryphal perhaps, nevertheless illustrates the process by which an immigrant might acquire a new identity. A German Jew became so flustered by the impatient questioning of an inspector that when asked his name he sputtered, "Schoyn vergessen (I forget)." The inspector, not understanding Yiddish, but hearing the words, welcomed "Sean Ferguson" to America. Members of the same family often emerged from Ellis Island with different surnames. The similar sound of the Ukrainian "G" and English "H" and an inspector's poor penmanship, left half of one Ukrainian family named Heskes, and the other half named Gesker.

Immigration officers also had to listen closely and use their imaginations to determine the newcomer's destination in America. Frequently, the only information that an immigrant had about where he was going would be a crumpled scrap of paper upon which was scrawled an illegible address. Those headed for "Nugers" were fortunate if their inspector bothered to help them clarify where in New Jersey they hoped to go. Sometimes, a convenient substitute was provided by a frustrated inspector, merely complicating the newcomer's search for his family or friends.

Of the three to four hundred people per day who passed before immigration officers during peak years, 80 percent were admitted without difficulty. These fortunate ones returned to the first floor of the main building where they might be met by friends or relatives who accompanied them on the ferryboat to New York. Others went to the railroad ticket office located on Ellis Island where they could purchase train tickets and await barges that would transport them to New Jersey railroad terminals for the last leg of their journey.

What of the unlucky 20 percent? Those not immediately admitted were detained on Ellis Island for various lengths of time, often in compartments created with wire, clearly visible to all other newcomers. Conditions were cramped, often unsanitary and poorly ventilated. People slept in three-tiered steel bunks, set in long rows with narrow aisles between them. The space between tiers was about two feet and the air was steamy, especially on hot summer nights. Often the bunks became lice infested. Most of the people stopped by the inspectors were held for medical reasons. Some of the physically ill were hospitalized. About 1 percent, who had readily detectable physical and mental abnormalities, were reexamined. A Board of Inquiry was presented with the medical report of these detainees, and this board made the final decision on each immigrant's admissability. After 1903, boards of inquiry automatically excluded those immigrant detainees declared unfit by medical personnel.

Families were often separated when one or more members were rejected. In such cases, private charitable organizations often intervened to help. If a child under eleven years old was rejected, the child's mother was encouraged by such organizations to return also. One worker for the Hebrew Immigrant Aid Society recalled how sad she and her colleagues were when "a little immigrant" had to go back and be treated "on the other side." Return passage was free because the shipping company was held responsible for delivering a sick immigrant, "But they (the companies) were not responsible to bring them back here to this country, so the poor father had to again struggle and save and put penny to penny."

Immigrants who were penniless but claimed to have relatives or friends who would defray their expenses until they found jobs were not immediately admitted. These immigrants, often as many as 10 percent of annual arrivals, were held briefly until funds from their sponsors were received by letter or telegram. Often a financially well-off relative or friend would be notified and would come to Ellis Island to assist the newcomer. Women and children were those most frequently detained for inadequate funds. They were given a place to sleep in the detention dormitory and were urged to contact by letter those responsible for them. If no one arrived within a week, the detainees could apply to one of the many immigrant aid organizations for assistance or accept deportation.

Known criminals, those suspected of being contract

laborers, or those considered likely to become public charges received immediate hearings. By the 1890s, a federal law had been passed to protect the jobs and wage rates of American workers from the competition of foreign workers recruited in Europe and imported by American businessmen. A tricky question asked of each immigrant concerned his employment status: if he said he lacked any job prospects, he risked being deported as likely to become a public charge. Immigrants learned from the sad experiences of others to say only that they had "good prospects" or "a relative's promise" of a job. If declared unfit for admission, such immigrants were returned to their port of departure within two weeks.

While the statistics on detentions are fragmentary, they suggest that a very modest percentage of immigrants were turned back at Ellis Island, despite rumors and anxieties generated by the inspection process. The total number of detentions in all categories was often as high as 20 percent on an annual basis, but over half of those detained were held only temporarily for minor health problems or until funds arrived. Only about 1 percent of the annual total were hospitalized and rarely did Board-of-Inquiry detentions exceed 10 percent. In 1907, a peak immigration year, there were 195,540 detentions as compared to a total of 1,004,756 admissions. Of those stopped, 121,737 were temporarily detained, 64,510 were held for specific inquiry, and 9,203 were hospitalized. Board-of-Inquiry exclusions comprised approximately 15 percent of the total cases heard. The individual immigrant arriving at Ellis Island need not have feared. Admission was the rule and rejection the exception.

Occasionally, corrupt immigration officials engaged in exploitation. In the summer of 1901, a scandal erupted involving the issuance of fraudulent naturalization papers which permitted those who could afford a five dollar fee to land directly from their ships and bypass Ellis Island. This and other outrages caused President Theodore Roosevelt to appoint William Williams, a tough young Wall Street lawyer and former government employee, Commissioner of Immigration at Ellis Island. Williams dressed his own agents, many of them friends from Wall

Street invited for the occasion, as immigrants and allowed them to undergo the full inspection procedure to smoke out the dishonest or inefficient. Many of the concessionaires, who had been bilking the newcomers, were ousted. A lucrative contract to exchange foreign currency was taken from a firm of swindlers and later given to the highly reputable American Express Company, which exchanged currency and sold railroad tickets.

Immigrants were as often cheated by those purporting to be their friends as they were by immigration officials. Shyster lawyers often took advantage of the formal examination procedures, the boards of inquiry, and the increasingly strict criteria for admission to gouge immigrants of their savings, even victimizing those of their own ethnic group. The immigration bureau ruled that lawyers could charge no more than ten dollars to represent a detained client at a hearing, but abuses were frequent. Dishonest merchants and confidence men also approached the new immigrants before they left Ellis Island. Criminals dressed as police officers or immigration inspectors sold newcomers phony licenses and official papers which they insisted the immigrant could not do without.

Social reformers and religious missionaries maintained a constant presence on Ellis Island to protect bewildered foreigners from scoundrels. Most missionaries represented a particular Protestant denomination or a nondenominational benevolent society. The Salvation Army, the Women's Home Missionary Society, and the New York Bible Society were among those represented. In 1907, the Industrial Committee of the Y.M.C.A. established a comprehensive immigration program and placed agents in major foreign ports and on board many ships as well as on Ellis Island. All societies were investigated by the federal government before being permitted to station representatives at the immigration depot. Only upon the recommendation of the Commissioner of Immigration did aid societies receive permission to visit detention rooms and interview detained immigrants. Representatives of these organizations were prohibited from securing the admittance of an alien through misrepresentations to inspectors at boards of inquiry and were forbidden to accept remuneration from immigrants for their services.

Many of the denominational societies were also warned not to attempt to convert beleaguered travelers. The American Tract Society was cautioned by immigration officials not to force Christian tracts, written in Hebrew or in Yiddish, on east European Jews landing at Ellis Island. One Commissioner of Immigration explained the rationale for the warning: "A great many of our immigrants are Hebrews, who are on their way from persecution by one style of Christians, and when they have Christian tracts—printed in Hebrew—put in their hands, apparently with the approval of the United States government, they wonder what is going to happen to them there."

The ethnic organizations made certain that the insults suffered by the members of their respective groups were called to the attention of immigration officials for appropriate action. Such organizations as St. Raphael's Society, the Society for the Protection of Italian Immigrants, and the Hebrew Immigrant Aid Society (HIAS) were highly respected by immigration officials, not only for their vigilance, but for their active assistance.

The activities of HIAS workers suggest how such ethnic societies served their own. Men and women wearing blue caps embroidered with the letters HIAS in Yiddish met the ferryboats landing at Ellis Island. They distributed to Jewish immigrants information sheets printed in Yiddish which explained the inspection procedures. They eased the fears of the anxious with warm smiles and advice on how to answer questions. And the immigrants asked them many questions: Should one lie or tell the truth? Should one claim poverty or show one's money? Would the immigration inspectors expect bribes such as those Russian officials had demanded? Society agents urged the immigrants to be honest and interceded with immigration officials so that the nervous, confused immigrant might have adequate opportunity to provide the correct information.

HIAS prosecuted swindlers who tried to exploit the naive and ran an employment bureau that remained open "every night except Friday." Newspapers would be brought by HIAS workers to Ellis Island on the ferry and all-night staff members would work to match each immigrant to a job advertisement. By World War I, HIAS had grown from a small, welfare society financed by a handful of benefactors, into a large organization with a nationwide membership, world-wide affiliates, and offices in Washington, D.C., and all major port cities. Still, until the tide of east European Jewish immigration ebbed in the 1920s, Ellis Island remained a major focus of HIAS activities.

If most immigrants were admitted to the United States, why were the hours on Ellis Island so often looked back upon, even by those who passed unhindered, as the worst experience of their lives? The testimony of those who endured the "Island of Tears" and are now Americans suggests that they were not timorous but had good reason for being unsure of themselves upon arrival. First, this was the initial official contact between the newcomers and America. The immigrants, already exhausted by their journey, were often confused by the procedures and intimidated by the cold, unfamiliar manner of immigration officials who did not speak their language or share their past. Second, many immigrants associated these new law enforcement officials with those whom they had feared in their home countries. This antipathy toward government officials was part of the emotional baggage borne by many new arrivals. They wondered whether American officials expected bribes as had those in their native lands; they had no idea what limits were set on the authority of these new officials. Third, the separation of families and detention of some immigrants moved even those not affected. And finally, many experienced a wrenching moment of panic that life was the same everywhere and that the hazards of their homeland were present in America; perhaps they had journeyed halfway around the globe for nothing.

Viewing their treatment on Ellis Island through a veil of past abuses and immediate anxieties, most immigrants perceived themselves to have been treated more harshly than in reality they were. One might also speculate that immigrants who recalled Ellis Island fifty years or more after being there remembered it as more brutal than it seemed even at the time because to do so enhanced their own achievement in surmounting the final obstacle between themselves and America.

Millions of men and women who had made the conscious decision to depart for America arrived on Ellis Island anxious to enter, but unprepared for the final hurdle. Even here, however, shrewd and resourceful immigrants, though unfamiliar with the language, culture, and law of their new country seized the initiative. They asked questions of those who had been through the process before; sought the advice of those who represented immigrant aid societies; and, in general, refused to capitulate to their own fears of America and the strange greeting it tendered. As they left Ellis Island the immigrants could congratulate themselves. They had survived their first encounter with American officialdom and gained valuable experience in coping with their new home.

I I I

The confusion of Ellis Island behind them, the new immigrants faced a myriad of fresh decisions which would shape their lives in the United States. A first choice concerned where in this strange, new country they would live and work. With few exceptions most newcomers congregated in cities, many never leaving the port city in which they landed. Unlike earlier immigrants, the latest settlers soon found that their own skills and preferences, as well as the state of the American economy, combined to make them urban dwellers.

The old immigrants of northwestern Europe who had arrived in mid-nineteenth century America came to a rural society of farms and small towns. German and Scandinavian immigrants often arrived with the minimum capital necessary to buy inexpensive tracts of prime farmland in Iowa, Wisconsin, Minnesota, and other states of the north-central United States. For those unable or unwilling to farm, new towns and cities of the west had provided abundant markets for peddlers, small merchants, or artisans. The Irish, most of whom had arrived with little money, capitalized on their brawn. They labored for low wages, building the canals and railroads which linked the farms of the hinterland with the markets and ports in the East. By the end of the century, however, American society had taken a new turn. America's workbenches were no longer mostly in Europe, but in her own cities.

The metamorphosis of a rural, agrarian society into an urban, industrial one had begun before the Civil War, but the pace of change had quickened considerably by the end of the nineteenth century. Inexpensive land that had attracted earlier immigrants was no longer available in abundance. Nor was there a need for vast quantities of laborers, whether skilled or unskilled, in the towns of rural America. However, such labor was needed in the growing industrial centers of the East and Middle West and in the mine fields that yielded the natural resources which nourished the city's factories.

The first to heed the siren call of the city were rural Americans unsettled by an agricultural depression in the 1870s and attracted by the sheen of urban life. The depopulation of the countryside was especially noticeable in the Middle West and the North Atlantic states. Between 1880 and 1890, more than half the towns in Iowa and Illinois declined in population, yet both states gained substantially in their overall number of inhabitants. In New England, 932 out of 1502 towns, including two-thirds of those in Maine and New Hampshire and three-fourths of those in Vermont, declined in population during the 1880s. However, the region actually gained 20 percent in total population through urban growth. Thousands of farms were abandoned and houses left to decay. Farmers who left the country for the city were met there by the new immigrants, who also hoped to find a niche in urban America.

The attitude of new immigrants toward life in this urban, industrialized society was shaped by each group's old-world experience and the nature of its aspirations. Only a small percentage of newcomers were disappointed to find that there was no longer an abundance of cheap land available. Most were glad to escape from the countryside.

Many groups, including the Italians, Slavs, and Greeks, rejected agrarianism and consciously chose to settle in cities. Oscar Handlin claimed that immigrants missed working the land, over which they "once bent in piety." However, more recent research disputes Handlin's contention. Joseph Lopreato, who has studied Italian settlement patterns, suggests that their old-world experience left most Italian immigrants feeling that farming was a punishment, for both stomach and soul. In southern Italy, the contadino's dependence upon agriculture had, according to Lopreato, "reduced him nearly to the status of the donkey and goat." Many newcomers considered themselves finally liberated from the soil and would not return to it.

Efforts to divert the flow of Italian immigrants from congested urban areas proved largely unsuccessful. The United States government, the Italian government, and a variety of state governments and private agencies encouraged the development of agricultural settlements for Italian immigrants in Texas, Arkansas, Alabama, Mississippi, and Louisiana. However, with few notable exceptions, these experiments failed. The gentry in Italy had not farmed and neither would the transplanted Italian farm worker. Wealth, power, prestige, and all worldly comforts were associated with a nonagrarian lifestyle. John W. Briggs (*An Italian Passage,* 1978) found that those Italians with the will and resources to emigrate came largely from "the upper levels of the working classes in the town and from the middle range of agriculturalists." Though his data are limited to the emigrants of only three communities—Termini, Serradifalco, and Villa Vallelonga—they are nevertheless suggestive. Italians already removed from the soil may well have viewed farming in America as a step backward socially.

A handful of Italians did go west and thrive, as Andrew F. Rolle has noted in *The Immigrant Upraised* (1968). Even Rolle admits, however, that most Italians did not venture beyond city limits. Those who did, he claims, were rewarded with greater prosperity and more rapid assimilation than their city cousins. However, most Italian immigrants preferred the safety and support of residence in an Italian urban enclave, and many regarded a move west as impractical because they intended their stay in America to be temporary.

Polish immigrants scattered across three dozen states and thousands of American communities. Most were concentrated in the industrial cities of the Great Lakes Basin—from New York to Illinois—but at least a third of the total lived in small, rural towns and villages. The American Polonia, as the immigrants referred to their presence in the United States, was not a tightly knit geographical entity. Wherever they lived, most Poles planned only to remain long enough to earn high wages and return to Poland. Therefore, most preferred the higher salaries of the coal mines of Scranton, Pennsylvania; the stockyards of Chicago, Illinois; the steelworks of Buffalo, New York. Only after many Poles settled permanently in their American homes, did some seek to buy land for cultivation. With little capital and the high price of land, those who preferred farming often became truck farmers serving a local market.

The character of Polish urbanism was often derived from noneconomic priorities, especially Catholicism. Since the vast majority of Polish immigrants were Roman Catholics, they tried to organize a parish as soon as possible after arrival and live in close proximity to it. Poles themselves often called their communities by parish names. In Polish, adding the suffix *owo* to a parish name formed a community name. Thus, in Chicago the Polish community near St. Stanislaus Kosta Church became the *Stanislawowo* or "St. Stanislaus District."

As did the majority of Italians and Poles, most Greeks settled in urban areas, either in the mill towns of New England or large northern cities such as New York and Chicago, where they worked in factories or found jobs as busboys, dishwashers, bootblacks, and peddlers. A somewhat less popular alternative was to go west. By 1907, there were already between thirty and forty thousand Greeks west of the Mississippi. In the Rocky Mountain region, Greek workers became the miners and smelters of Colorado and Utah. In California especially, but in other states as well, they worked on railroad gangs. Fewer Greeks settled in the South; only one in fifteen settled in one of the old Confederacy's eleven states. The South offered little industrial employment or commercial opportunity, so Greeks who went there frequently carried with them sufficient capital for a restaurant, fruit store, or shoe shine parlor. Greeks did create economic opportunity for their fellow immigrants such as in Tarpon Springs, Florida, where John Cocoris and his brothers organized a sponge business. They brought five hundred Greeks from the Aegean and Dodecanese Islands to dive, hook, clean, sort, string, clip, and pack. Tarpon Springs remained America's sponge center and a Greek mecca until after World War II. However, most Greek immigrants cared little for sponges and even less for lives of rural isolation, choosing a city as their American address, while they saved for the day when they could return to Greece.

Most new immigrants, then, rejected agriculture and rural life in America, at least initially. These immigrants consciously chose to remain in the port city where they disembarked or to journey inland to another urban area, often joining family or friends in an ethnic enclave, where they could create a new world on their own terms.

Many of the hardships that immigrants suffered initially were also shared by those native Americans who came to the city during the late nineteenth and early twentieth centuries. Most American cities were ill-equipped to sustain the vast multitudes of new residents—foreign and native born—descending upon them. Transportation, housing, sanitation, and health facilities constructed in a preindustrial age for smaller populations were inadequate to meet the needs of burgeoning urban populations. In New York City, the foreign-born population skyrocketed from 567,812 in 1870 to 902,643 in 1890, yet declined from 38 percent of the total population to 36 percent. By 1910, the figure was almost 2,000,000 (still only 41 percent of the total). Quite obviously, the city was being filled just as quickly from the hinterland as from the docks.

The strain placed upon city services and facilities by these new urban dwellers was unanticipated. When the new immigration began in the 1880s, residents of major American port cities depended upon facilities that had been planned and built before the Civil War and were already outdated. In *Boss Tweed's New York* (1965), Seymour Mandelbaum's description of city streets rendered impassable by the sheer volume of traffic suggests that even the nation's largest city was unprepared for the new demands made upon its antiquated design:

No one moved above the streets, no one below them. Vehicles of every description and function crowded together in the same narrow thoroughfares. There were no limited-access highways, no special truck routes. No Manhattan rail connections served the docks. Cargo and passengers were forced into the same struggling line of movement. Wooden planks split under the pressure of a business traffic for which they were never intended. Cobblestones were torn loose faster than they could be replaced.

As the immigrants, fresh from the docks themselves, found their way uptown, they needed only to glance at their shoes or take deep breaths to realize that America had yet to master the problems of densely populated industrial cities. Filth year round and, in winter, ice and snow accumulated on city streets. Not all streets were paved, and those that were surfaced were cleaned by private companies under contract to the city. When funds were in short supply, streets were neglected for weeks at a time. Sewage presented an even greater problem. Prior to 1865, city sewers were a patchwork of pipelines set down by private property owners without any central coordination. By the end of the century, these pipes were too narrow to handle the increasing load. Those improperly laid often burst. Mains opened into the rivers at many points, rather than at a few central spots. In the older parts of cities, where immigrants usually found their first homes, clogged mains frequently caused sewers to overflow, flooding the streets with waste. After a heavy rainstorm, city streets with improper drainage became little lakes of brown mud and slime.

Tired of wading through mud or of being jostled on congested streets, the newly arrived immigrants might board streetcars. In the late nineteenth century, horse-drawn vehicles were rapidly being replaced by electric trolleycars, while in New York a vast elevated and underground train system was under construction. Prior to consolidation and public financing in any cities, streetcars were owned and operated by private companies. Competitive lines crowded close to one another along routes where the demand for transportation promised highest profits. Without the planning of municipal government, chaotic distribution of lines by entrepreneurs left whole areas of the city isolated from one another. Traveling at four to six miles per hour, street cars hardly provided rapid transit, even if a rider found one going in just the right direction.

Whether they walked or rode, the new immigrants' first priority was to find food and shelter. Those settling in New York, Chicago, or any other large city would not necessarily have found their first American home in one of the towering tenements that have come to symbolize the immigrant experience. Despite an acute shortage of housing for the urban poor reaching back decades, tenements were not built in large numbers until the early 1880s. At first, single family wooden houses were converted into apartment buildings. Some of the larger houses became the first urban tenements.

New immigrants, such as the Slavs and the Greeks, who often labored in mines or on construction sites, lived in nearby shacks that soon became part of scattered shanty towns. According to Victor R. Greene in *The Slavic Community on Strike* (1968), permanent residents in the anthracite coal country of Pennsylvania referred to the group of shacks where the Polish and Lithuanian miners lived as the Slavic mining "patch." Shacks resembled in many ways the peasant cottages the immigrant had left behind in Poland. Crowded within were the owner, the family, and frequently several male boarders, who wanted the least expensive lodgings. Lucky was the immigrant who found such lodging and did not have to sleep outdoors as did many who were unable to find affordable shelter.

Less fortunate immigrants were frequently exploited by non-Slavic landlords, frequently Irish or English, who crammed as many as eleven people into one-room cellars, eleven feet square; or twenty-one into a two-storied stable, sixteen by fourteen; or six men into a room without ventilation that measured only fourteen by nine feet. Improvement came when the family could buy or rent land for their own one-room shanty. Shanties were built with whatever material was available, such as railroad ties, timber, driftwood, and empty tin cans. An addition or a second story might later be built for boarders.

The tenement was born of a desire to squeeze greater profits from limited space. As Moses Rischin has noted, "New York's division of city lots into standard rectangular plots, 25 feet by 100 feet deep made decent human accommodation impossible." Builders found themselves unable to allow for proper light and ventilation and still provide profitable housing to meet the great demand created by the new immigration. The result was the construction of blocks and blocks of dumbbell-style tenements.

At first glance, the tall tenements appeared to loom romantically against the sky. Novelist and social critic William Dean Howells (*Impressions and Experiences,* 1896) admired the structures from afar but changed his mind after entering one:

But to be in it, and not have the distance, is to inhale the stenches of the neglected street, and to catch the yet fouler and dreadfuller poverty-smell which breathes from the open doorways. . . . It is to see the work-worn look of mothers, the squalor of the babies, the haggish ugliness of the old women, and the slovenly frowsiness of the young girls.

Even those who, like Howells, saw romance in silhouettes of tenements, soon agreed with the author who said that, "had the foul fiend designed these great barricades they could not have been more villainously arranged to avoid any change of ventilation. . . ."

Each end of the six- or seven-story, dumbbell-shaped structure was composed of four apartments to a floor, two on either side of a separating corridor. The front apartments generally contained four rooms each, while the back apartments had three rooms each. Only a single room in each apartment received direct light and air from the street or from the required ten feet of yard space at the back of each tenement. Often there were two stores on the ground floor with a small apartment behind each. These rooms received little light but adequate air from windows facing airshafts. The airshafts, five feet wide and sixty feet deep, separated the tenement building. Toilets were communal, four per floor, located off the airshafts. The lack of public toilets forced residents away from home to use vacant lots or, in the evening, the sides of wagons. The streets stank and summers were especially unbearable. Tenement dwellers sought to escape the heat of their apartments and the smells of the street below by moving mattresses onto roofs and fire escapes.

In a fire, tenements became death-traps. Of the 250 recorded deaths in Manhattan fires between 1902 and 1909, one-third were Lower East Side victims of tenement fires. Often families cramped for space had cut off their own paths of escape by piling furniture and belongings onto fire escapes.

Most families could not afford the privacy of their own three- or four-room apartment, but lodgers or boarders who required little space made the monthly rent of ten to twenty dollars more affordable. Still, the precariousness of the immigrants' economic conditions often ended in an eviction. Some years, over ten thousand eviction notices were issued to residents of Manhattan's Lower East Side.

Tenements of the dumbbell variety provided landlords with handsome annual profits. Immigrants, leery of contact with authorities, permitted landlords to blatantly ignore health and housing laws. Not until municipal governments, pressured by urban reformers, outlawed dumbbell tenements were some abuses corrected. In New York, the Tenement House Law of 1901 established new guidelines for builders. All new buildings had to have windows opening a minimum of twelve feet from the building opposite it. Each unit had to have its own toilet and running water, clear access to fire-escapes, and sturdy staircases. Older buildings had to undergo alterations, at least to the extent of installing modern toilet facilities. A Tenement House Department was organized in New York to enforce the new legislation, but inefficiency and corruption plagued its operation. At best, the legislation was an acknowledgement of the threat that tenements posed to the health and safety of occupants, most of whom were immigrants.

Urban immigrants, staring through smudged windows to the airshaft wall, rarely had a balanced diet, often scarcely any food at all. The newly landed immigrants found American food much too expensive. Their diet was frequently heavy with starches and fats, and low on protein. Italians ate bread, potatoes, some eggs, fish, and pasta. Slavs and East European Jews subsisted for days on herring, bread, and tea, with potatoes, and cheap meats such as lung among other staples. Greeks ate sausage with rice, potatoes, eggs, lentils, or greens during the week. Only on occasional Sundays did they enjoy the luxury of soups or a roast. In *The Bitter Cry of the Children* (1906), reformer John Spargo observed that, among some immigrants, long periods without nutritious food caused children to develop stomachs "too weak by reason of chronic hunger and malnutrition to stand good and nutritious food."

The clamoring demand for inexpensive food tempted some businessmen to cut costs by ignoring health standards. Upton Sinclair's novel, *The Jungle* (1905), chronicles the exposure of Jurgis Rudders, a Lithuanian immigrant, to the exploitation and depravity of the meat-packing industry in Chicago. However, the food industry also offered honest prosperity to those catering to their own ethnic groups' preferences or ritual necessities. Food stores often broadened their stock to include items geared toward attracting the patronage of specific immigrants.

The new immigrants adjusted their diets even as they accommodated themselves to the rigors of life in the American communities where they settled. They had already chosen to leave their homes and families in search of greater prosperity. They had survived the trauma of departure and the trials of the journey, using the ruses and resources at their command to surmount natural and man-made obstacles. The sea and Ellis

Island's inspectors were behind them, but much remained to test the fortitude and perseverance of the immigrants.

With the United States in the midst of rapid industrialization and increasing urbanization, newcomers as well as natives found in cities the most plentiful opportunities for economic advancement—but there was a price. For immigrants the cost was often physical deprivation and psychological strain as they pitted their sagacity against the jarring reality of a strange, sometimes hostile environment. Appetizing food and affordable housing were scarce in congested cities designed for the smaller populations of a preindustrial order. It was the economic magnet of employment and good wages that had drawn immigrants to American cities, or the towns near mills and mines. However, it was largely the particular ethnic backgrounds and old-world experiences of immigrants that would shape their choice of jobs and the character of their neighborhoods.

THREE

Smokestacks and Pushcarts: Work and Mobility in Industrial America

The new immigrants in the United States faced the difficult task of carving for themselves a niche in a society to which they were strangers. What could they do here? What did they have that America needed? They soon discovered that there were an abundance of jobs for new immigrants in the American economy. The rapid industrialization of the United States in the years following the Civil War had created a demand for cheap, unskilled labor. Newcomers could quickly find employment after leaving the immigration depot or crossing the border.

Two antithetical images characterize the popular perception of immigrants in the American economy. One suggests a cluster of creative, ambitious, and optimistic individuals relieved to be in America and ready to take advantage of every opportunity to follow in the footsteps of Horatio Alger's heroes on the path from rags to riches. The inverse portrays immigrants as a faceless mass of unskilled labor, sadistically exploited by robber baron industrialists for their own profit and the ultimate benefit of American industry. In mine and sweatshop, according to this view, newcomers gained little besides physical hardship and psychological humiliation until rescued by the rise of labor unions. In more recent media creations, long-oppressed immigrant workers spontaneously sprout radical consciences and demand mid-twentieth century versions of social justice minutes after witnessing the Triangle Shirtwaist fire or the bloody repercussions of a mineworkers' strike.

In reality, immigrants did not have a uniform reaction to the American economy. Both in background and goals, the newcomers varied by ethnic group and as individuals within groups. Even for those without capital or skills, opportunities were available. Native Americans grudgingly curbed their prejudices against various immigrant groups whenever the need for the newcomers' labor seemed paramount. Thus, necessity offered to the newcomers opportunities which prejudice might have withheld. Occupation and success, then, were neither absolutely predetermined by the immigrant's past nor limited by an inflexible class system, but molded by individual choice and the economic laws of supply and demand.

New immigrants arrived with economic attitudes and values tucked among their cultural baggage, thus it is essential to examine their economic behavior in the light of their past and not against the yardstick of American conceptions of mobility alone. Historian James A. Henretta contends that Americans are judged upwardly mobile by other Americans if they can rise above their neighbors within a society that values and sustains open competition. Not all new immigrants shared with Americans this basic perception of mobility. Economic behavior accepted as appropriate by natives of agricultural societies with seasonal, family-oriented patterns of work was often perceived as laziness by Americans. Upward mobility, then, cannot be divorced in discussion from its cultural context among new immigrant peoples.

Economically ambitious immigrants sought out others in their ethnic group who shared this emphasis on upward mobility. They often created mutual benevolence societies to generate economic assistance among themselves. The *ken* and *hui* organizations of Japanese and Chinese immigrants, respectively, were often the means whereby immigrants progressed economically, drawing upon the advice, encouragement, and even capital of other group members. These voluntary societies were often the mechanism for reconciling new-world needs and old-world economic patterns.

I

Most new immigrants entered the American economy through the factories and mines of the northeastern United States, the hub of America's industry. Eighty percent of the new immigrants remained in the northeast. Their settlement patterns formed a triangle: New England was at the apex, with the southeastern point at Washington, D.C., and the southwestern point at St. Louis. Two-thirds of all the immigrants could be found in New York, the New England states, Pennsylvania, and New Jersey, while substantial numbers also went west to Illinois and Ohio. Few immigrants ventured into the southern states as industry was still scarce there. Immigrants who landed in southern ports and chose to remain faced job competition from low-paid native white and black laborers. Fear of discrimination dissuaded many dark-complexioned immigrants from settling in the south, except for the more cosmopolitan port cities such as New Orleans and Charleston.

The major cities of the North—New York, Philadelphia, Baltimore, Boston, and Chicago—were attractive to newcomers. Jobs for the unskilled were plentiful in these industrial centers, and the presence of compatriots often helped newcomers adjust quickly to the daily rhythms of life in America.

Caroline Golab, in *Immigrant Destinations* (1978), pointed out that these older cities remained centers of commerce into the late nineteenth century and early twentieth, and "continued to support what had once been the nation's handicrafts and household industries—the making of clothes, shoes, silverware, wooden toys and the like." Thus, there were opportunities for skilled artisans and craftsmen as well as unskilled laborers. In turn, the high concentrations of population in these cities provided a market for small merchants.

Some older cities actually became cities of immigrants. According to the census records of 1910, about 75 percent of the populations of New York, Chicago, Detroit, Cleveland, and Boston were made up of immigrants or their children. Many of these were the offspring of earlier settlers such as the Irish and Germans, but most were new immigrants from southern and eastern Europe or Canada. Foreign enclaves of sizable proportion were also located in Philadelphia and Providence— industrial cities linked to the nation's expanding industrial network by rail. In the West, the port city of San Francisco was particularly popular with immigrants, especially those from China and Japan. By 1916, over 72 percent of the population in that city regarded a foreign language as their primary tongue.

New immigrant groups concentrated in regions where there were opportunities that matched the capabilities and cultural preferences of their members. The Slavic groups settled in the mining and industrial regions of Ohio, Illinois, Michigan, New York, and large areas of western Pennsylvania. They were also predominant in the labor force of Chicago's slaughterhouses and worked on construction sites throughout the northeast.

According to one observer, the Slavs were considered desirable workers because of "their habit of silent submission, their amenability to discipline, and their willingness to work long hours and overtime without a murmur." The *Pittsburgh Leader* testified that the east European immigrant made "a better slave than the American."

Victor Greene, who has studied the Slavic community in the anthracite coal region of Pennsylvania, suggests that such observations were based on a thorough misconception of the goals and values of these immigrants. The Slavs were "birds of passage" who viewed their stay in America as a brief visit to last only long enough for them to earn money with which to purchase land in their native countries. Slavs as a group were the most physically robust of the new immigrants, and were willing to tolerate the wretched working conditions of the mines in exchange for wages higher than in other industries. Emily Balch who studied the Slavs in 1910 noted that even among the unskilled who spoke little English, miners were better paid than mill workers, receiving $2.40 to $3.00 for eight hours in the Pittsburgh mines as compared to $2.28 to $2.41 for a twelve hour day in the mills.

Slavic laborers willingly tolerated wretched working conditions, provided that wages were high, because they regarded their stay in the United States as temporary—even after they had, in fact, become permanent residents. One Polish imigrant recalled that at the beginning of this century her parents had left her and her siblings in Poland when they came to work in America, "They both came with the idea that they're both gonna make a little money and go back, finish that new house. And of course we were there. . . ." However, even as they talked of returning, a growing family and other circumstances kept her parents in America. "But the children kept comin' every twenty months here; then the war (World War I) broke out, so they stayed. . . ." (June Namias, ed., *First Generation,* 1978). Historians have often mistakenly assessed Slavic behavior as if the Slavs knew they would never return, rather than from the perspective that the Slavs had of their condition at the time. The change in Slavic reaction to unionization, discussed more fully later in this chapter, suggests a shift in perspective. Slavs resisted unions as long as they planned to return home. However, once they realized they would be staying in America, they became amenable to organization.

Those Slavs who arrived with some capital often elected to purchase or rent small plots of land in the Northeast or Midwest. About one-third of the Poles to arrive in the United States engaged in truck farming in these regions. On New York's Long Island, Polish truck farmers grew tomatoes and other vegetables. In the Connecticut Valley, they cultivated tobacco, onions, and asparagus; and in the north central Midwest, they planted corn and wheat.

Like the Slavs, many Italian immigrants planned to be "birds of passage" and acquire enough money to return to their home villages with status and wealth. Males often arrived in large numbers in the early spring, finding jobs on construction gangs and living sparsely until the late fall. They spent the winter months in Italy to return the following spring. Families came later, once a little money had been accumulated, or when it was apparent that being strangers in the United States was preferable to being political and social peons in the Mezzogiorno.

Arriving with strong backs, few skills, and little or no capital, most Italians turned to manual labor wherever they settled. In New York, Italian labor built the subways and some of the bridges linking the boroughs. In 1897, over 75 percent of the workers on New York City construction projects were Italian. They rolled cigars by hand in Florida. They groomed the grape vineyards in California. On the prairies they laid the track linking coast to coast. Though many worked in factories, especially in New England textile mills and New York garment factories, most Italian males preferred working outdoors. Those Italian women who joined the work force took up the jobs as factory operatives.

Josef Barton's study of Italians, Romanians, and Slovaks in Cleveland (*Peasants and Strangers,* 1975) suggests that those immigrants who had developed skills as artisans or merchants in their home culture adapted most easily to urban environments in the United States. Barton observed that among Italians, social background prior to emigration "strongly influenced both their first job and their subsequent work experience." Italian immigrants had not all been peasants or fishermen. Those from certain social milieux were better prepared than others to enter America's industrialized economy. Almost half of the artisans traced by Barton, for example, entered skilled positions after emigration to the United States, and an additional 40 percent found their first jobs in white-collar occupations. Moreover, artisans experienced the most important long-term gains. Twenty years after their arrival in Cleveland, almost two-thirds of all Italian artisans studied by Barton were middle class. Laborers and peasants, and their sons, had much greater difficulty transforming themselves into prosperous Americans.

Italians who had been laborers in Italy often retained old work habits and preferences in their new American environment. They preferred jobs with steady hours and a set salary to jobs that offered rapid advancement at the price of irregular or excessive hours of labor. Work was important, but must not intrude upon family life, especially upon the interaction of parents and children. Social historian Stephan Thernstrom (*The Other Bostonians,* 1973) suggests that Italians—even in the second generation—were frequently unfamiliar with "the idea that work can be a central purpose of life, and that it should be organized into a series of related jobs that make up a career . . ." There was little hunger for promotions or fear of loss of face if they became plasterers or plumbers rather than professionals or independent entrepreneurs.

Unlike rural Italians who sent males first, Italian fishermen often emigrated with their families and thus were better able to deal with the dislocation and disruption of traditional life-patterns in the cities of America. Often Sicilian fishermen and their sons made remarkably rapid adjustments to American urban life because a fishing job in the Mediterranean was a business enterprise. After a catch, fishermen had always marketed their wares directly to consumers.

Like the Italians, Greek immigrants preferred outdoor work but generally avoided agriculture. Only a few turned to farming or herding and migrated to the western states, where, according to Theodore Saloutos, "The mountains, valleys, shores, and skies reminded them of their birthplaces." Most became laborers in factories or worked on railroad construction gangs, where they could at least remain out of doors. The textile mills of New England, long a source of jobs for immigrants, also attracted many Greeks. By 1910, Lowell, Massachusetts, had 20,000 Greeks among its 100,000 inhabitants. Following earlier waves of Irish and French Canadians into the mills, Greeks underbid the wages of their predecessors and had the reputation for being less inclined to drink and therefore more reliable laborers. Wages were low, less than four dollars per week, but the work was steady.

The areas of settlement and occupational preferences of east European Jews were also affected by a combination of historic experience, cultural preferences, expectations, and individual abilities. Unlike most of the Slavic, Italian, and Greek immigrants mentioned above, Jews arriving at the turn of the century tended to be skilled artisans or experienced merchants. Because many east European countries had laws proscribing Jews from owning land, they frequently developed nonagrarian skills easily transferrable should it become necessary to move quickly. Since medieval times, Jews had been moneylenders, tax collectors, innkeepers, grain merchants, stewards, artisans, and commercial middlemen. In the Pale, Jews predominated among the tanners, tailors, blacksmiths, carpenters, furriers, jewelers, bakers, and butchers. By 1900, many eastern European towns had workshops and sweatshops where varied craftsmen worked side by side to produce ready-made goods for the urban market. Many Jews were retailers, peddlers, and shopkeepers. And even before the turn of the century, Jews constituted over a fifth of the factory operatives in the Pale of Russia and almost 28 percent in Poland.

Sixty-six percent of the Jewish males who arrived in the United States between 1899 and 1914 were classified as skilled workers compared to an average of 20 percent for all other male immigrants combined. For Jewish immigrants then, the transition from their cities and villages to the urban industrial centers of the United States was eased because they carried with them valuable skills. Jews who had been tailors in rural villages or labored in town workshops found a ready place in New York's garment industry. They dominated the industry, doing piecework in their tenement apartments on their own sewing machines or on machines rented from employers. In such cases every family member regardless of age or sex contributed his or her labor. Thus, in New York City the garment industry employed approximately 50 percent of all the city's Jewish males and two-thirds of the city's Jewish wage-earners. In New York and other port cities, Jewish workers also found positions in cigar factories, print shops, and book binderies.

Just as cultural values brought from home villages influenced the occupational choices of male immigrants, so too they determined roles of immigrant women and children. All immigrants relied on the cooperation of family members, regardless of gender, to supplement the earnings of the male head of household, but the nature of that help varied from group to group.

The role of the immigrant woman worker especially has long been neglected by historians. Women were restricted in their occupations and working conditions by their particular group's cultural traditions and taboos and by the well-intentioned efforts of American reformers to protect all women from the evils of industrial exploitation. Women from the Mediterranean countries frequently helped their husbands or fathers sell goods at markets or peddle them in the streets. In small shops they might manage the bills and inventory. Slovak and Bohemian women did domestic work as had Irish women of a previous immigrant generation. However, Greek, Italian, and Jewish women were usually prohibited by their families from doing outside domestic work. These groups considered it demeaning for a woman to work in any household but her own. This taboo had nothing to do with the arduousness of the work. Women from these groups were permitted to become sewing machine operators in garment factories, and, by 1910, thousands of Greek women were laboring in New England's textile and shoe factories. In the southwest, Mexican women preferred jobs as domestics, but when such employment was unavailable they worked in the fields, as did the men.

Of course many young immigrant women were not under the supervision of a father or husband. Some had come alone to America. Others had been married, but were widowed or the victims of desertion. Some of these women, impoverished and unable to cope with the stresses of life in America, turned to the oldest profession for their livelihoods. Prostitutes were not confined to isolated corners of cities as they had been in eastern Europe or southern Italy. They lived in the same streets and in the same tenements where families lived and children cavorted. They were often regarded with a combination of shame and sympathy by their respective groups. Italians, Jews, and Slavs often blamed hardship in America for driving young, unmarried women to the streets.

Single women, though still constrained by old-world values and customs, and the circumscribed role that American society permitted its female members, did actively shape their own lives. Labor organizer Rose Schneiderman, who arrived in 1889, recalled that, when her father died, her pregnant mother became the family's sole support. When the baby was weaned, Rose's mother took a job in a fur factory, leaving Rose to stay with the baby. Two other brothers were temporarily placed in the Hebrew Orphan Asylum. Later, her mother, concerned about Rose's schooling, sent her to the orphanage too. But within a year Rose and the baby were again living with their mother in a one-room apartment. Her mother worked all day and brought home bundles to sew at night. On weekends they visited the boys at the orphanage (Rose Schneiderman and Lucy Goldthwaite, *All for One,* 1967).

Young single women, especially among newly arrived Italians and Jews, often became active in labor organization. They were the backbone of the garment industry unions. Jewish immigrant women often emerged as leaders. Some had been active in the Jewish labor movement in Russia. At first the Yiddish speaking women trade unionists had difficulty communicating with their Italian co-workers. In 1907, an effort to organize artificial flower makers failed because the Italian immigrant women who dominated the industry could not understand the speeches of their union's leadership. One observer remarked that "the only time there was a large turnout for mass meetings was when English and Italian speakers were on the platform." Other cultural differences separated female immigrants as well. Meetings planned for Saturday nights interfered with Italian family homelife and were poorly attended. Also, Italian males often escorted their wives or sisters to and from work and intervened to "protect" their women from union organizers who, they feared, were keeping Italian women from home responsibilities. However, increasing contact bred understanding and by the turn of the century, Italian and Jewish immigrant women were in the vanguard of labor unionization in the garment trades.

Immigrant women of all groups found work in mills, canneries, tobacco factories, commercial laundries, and other occupations requiring quick hands and dexterity. Women too frail to work in factories or tied to their homes by the duties of motherhood frequently supplemented their family's income through boarders, collecting rent, cooking meals, and doing laundry for the renters. At times, such services yielded more income than the woman's husband made as a laborer.

State legislation limited the working hours for all women. The first such legislation was passed in New Hampshire as early as 1847, and by the turn of the century many other states had followed that state's example in response to pressure from social reformers. A law enacted in Oregan in 1903 provided that "no female (shall) be employed in any mechanical establishment, or factory or laundry in this State more than ten hours during any one day." The legislation was later upheld in the landmark case *Muller* v. *Oregon,* 1908. Louis Brandeis, arguing for the state, persuaded the Court that long hours impaired the health, safety, and morals of working women. The majority of the Supreme

Court concurred that women's "physical structure and a proper discharge of her maternal functions—having in view not merely her own health but the well-being of the race—justify the legislation to protect her from the greed as well as the passion of man." By 1913, thirty-nine states either enacted new legislation protecting women workers or improved legislation already enacted.

Enforcement of female labor legislation varied from state to state. Ironically, the efforts of social reformers often hurt those they were trying hardest to help—immigrant women. Wages were so low, and life so marginal, that limiting the hours of immigrant women workers frequently spelled economic disaster for the family. Thus, many immigrant women were forced to evade the very laws written to protect them. And they were readily aided in this by exploitative employers.

Child labor, like female labor, was initially determined by the cultural norms of each particular new immigrant group. Not until the twentieth century would the intervention of humanitarian reformers alter child employment patterns. According to Virginia Yans McLaughlin, in her 1977 study of immigrants in Buffalo, Italian girls rarely left home to accept jobs as domestics or factory laborers. Boys, however, could accept whatever kind of employment they were capable of performing. Older boys often duplicated their father's salaries in seasonal labor, while the younger ones worked in street trades as newsboys or shoeshiners. Among the Slavic miners, girls were permitted to work in local textile mills, while the boys went down into the mines as soon as they were able. Before the age of twelve, Slavic boys worked on the surface, but by their mid-teens they were riding the elevators below ground.

East European Jews generally preferred to keep daughters at home and permitted sons to work in shops and factories as they were able. However, the piecework that was available in the garment trades often permitted the entire family to work together. In 1902, reformer and journalist Hutchins Hapgood wrote in *Spirit of the Ghetto,* that the homes of Jews on New York's Lower East side were often turned into work rooms.

"During the day the front room, bedroom, and kitchen became a whirling, churning factory, where men, women and children worked at the sewing and pressing machines." Hapgood and others were often surprised and dismayed to see the extent to which child labor was used in homes and in factories, where young children worked elbow to elbow with adults under confined conditions. "In one room," Hapgood discovered, "would be four men, one or two women, a couple of young girls, aged nine to fourteen, and perhaps an eleven-year old boy, working on knickerbockers or knee pants." Another observer described how mothers, too busy sewing, often relegated to a female child "the work and care of the family . . . washing, scrubbing, cooking. . . ." Home labor, with everyone in the family employed, was often no more profitable than piecework in factories. Rapacious employers often reduced the amount paid for each finished piece. Workers were thereby forced to work faster and faster to receive the same low wage. By the 1920s, laws in most states fixed a minimum age for employment and compelled school attendance. Compliance was not immediate, but advancing mechanization, an adequate adult labor supply, and rising personnel standards in industry increasingly made child labor less profitable to employers. However, immigrant families in need of supplementary income continued to violate the law whenever economic necessity demanded.

II

By the turn of the century, then, the new immigrants were becoming the chief source of labor in almost every area of industrial production. Southern and eastern European languages and English spoken with the accents of the Mezzogiorno, eastern European villages, and French Canada echoed in factories and mines in concentrated regional pockets. The Dillingham Commission's report published in 1910 states that, in a twenty-one industry survey, it found that 57.9 percent of all employees were foreign-born, approximately two-thirds being of southern and eastern European origin. In industries such as garment manufacturing, coal mining, slaughtering, meat packing, construction, and confectionery, the proportion of new immigrant to native-born labor was even higher.

It is impossible to gauge precisely the immediate impact of a new immigrant labor force upon the American-born and the entrenched older immigrants. Nativist literature published after 1890 often suggested that new immigrant laborers were displacing American workers at every work site. Though not completely accurate, for particular industries, such as coal mining and iron and steel manufacturing, these charges do appear to have had some basis in fact. Low-paid Poles and Slavs were nudging out those of English or Irish heritage.

Rapid expansion of American industry kept foreign and American workers from actually colliding. Lateral movement and vertical promotion kept many native-born workers clear of the newcomers. New mines in the western states absorbed displaced miners from Pennsylvania and Ohio. Though the evidence is still vague and impressionistic, there is also some indication that American workers were elevated into managerial and technical positions created in industries by the growth that new immigrant labor helped generate. In some factories and plants, the native American managers and foremen owed a debt to the newcomers, whose presence was responsible for their own ascent into these white-collar jobs.

The availability of cheap immigrant labor afforded the United States a decided competitive advantage over its European industrial rivals. The owners of America's mines, large factories, and small sweatshops did not hesitate to exploit their inexpensive and abundant supply of immigrant labor. Twelve- to sixteen-hour days were normal in factories and mines. Unventilated shops, inadequate exhaust systems, and improper safety equipment exposed the workers to noxious fumes and other health hazards. Mine workers often died prematurely of lung diseases, while those in factories suffered loss of limbs or eyes in industrial accidents. While employers blamed workers' carelessness or inexperience for the accidents, investigators such as Cyril

Eastman, in 1910, pointed to ignored safety hazards and malfunctioning equipment. Workers injured on the job and unable to earn a living received no compensation. Medical or funeral expenses were left to impoverished workers and their families. Neither employers nor the government aided those unable to work as the result of sickness or industrial accidents.

The earliest attempts at labor organization were aimed as much against the immigrants as against exploitative employers. The huge pool of immigrant labor threatened to undermine the status of all American workers by rapidly decreasing wages and encouraging managers to think of employees as sometimes even more easily replaced than a piece of machinery. Organizations such as the National Labor Union, begun by iron-molder William Sylvis in 1868, and the Knights of Labor, founded in 1869, restricted their membership to workers skilled in a craft. Trained to work in an era prior to wide-scale mechanization, these workers were concerned with protecting the status and integrity of their particular craft. Specifically, they attempted to regulate the pace of production to allow for painstaking, high quality craftsmanship and to protect wages against immigrant competition.

Ironically, these labor organizations eventually were forced to turn to the immigrants for survival. Machines increasingly replaced the skilled craftsman, and industrialists were quick to realize that, whereas they were required to compensate each skilled employee individually commensurate with his abilities, they could impose a uniform set of hours, working conditions, and wages upon a production line. As their original membership slipped in status or became unemployed, labor groups had no choice but to court the millions of unskilled, immigrar* laborers.

The 1880s witnessed both extreme labor unrest and the emergence of a new type of labor union. In 1886, alone, an estimated 610,000 men and women were out of work because of strikes, lockouts, or shutdowns that sometimes erupted in violence. The extreme violence in the labor movement was epitomized by the Haymarket Riot in 1886. In Chicago, a city known for radical and anarchist activity, unemployed workers, many of whom were Irish and German immigrants, gathered for a rally in the city's Haymarket Square. Someone threw a bomb, killing a policeman and several bystanders. A bloody melee ensued. Club-swinging policemen waded into the crowd, injuring hundreds, and members of the crowd retaliated in kind. The police blamed the riot on eight alleged anarchists, most of whom were immigrants of German background. After jury trials, four of the eight were hanged. The terrible legacy of the Haymarket riot trials were associated in many American minds with the organized labor movement, immigrant workers, and dangerous wild-eyed radicals and anarchists. For many, the incident justified fears of the "reckless foreign wretches," as one newspaper termed the protesting workers.

Despite bad publicity generated by the Haymarket affair and other violent incidents, the American labor movement expanded and drew followers from among skilled workers both native and foreign-born during the last two decades of the nineteenth century. Especially attractive was the new American Federation of Labor (AFL) founded in 1881, which grew as the Knights of Labor declined in influence and membership. The AFL had recognized the unique problems affecting the workers in different occupations by encouraging the development of separate craft unions. It decided to represent all these unions, amassing strength in numbers while permitting each member union to preserve its autonomy, including the power to call strikes. Samuel Gompers, a Jewish immigrant born in London, became the first president of the AFL. For forty years he sought to win for organized labor recognition as a legitimate interest group within American society. More immediately, Gompers sought higher wages, shorter hours, and equitable treatment for the Federation's members.

The AFL was anxious to enlist new immigrants in the union movement, but most southern and eastern Europeans were unskilled laborers and thus ineligible for membership in a craft union. Even many of the skilled workers among the immigrants were difficult to recruit because of the system of home production popular among many groups. Workers performed piece-work on sewing machines or at work benches in their tenement apartments and delivered the completed pieces to sweatshops where the garment or other product was assembled. Union organizing committees lacked the manpower to go through apartment buildings door-to-door to reach such workers.

At first, many new immigrants rejected unions as irrelevant to their plans and expectations for the future. "Birds of passage" regarded their exposure to the injustices of the in-dustrial system as a temporary inconvenience. Others did not see themselves as an intrinsic part of American society until long after they settled here. And both national and regional dif-ferences kept workers apart. Businessmen anxious to break unions were quick to exploit these differences. In 1903, the first large group of Greek workers was sent west to break a strike of Italian coal miners in Utah. Nine years later, in 1912, striking Greek miners from the island of Crete clashed with mainland Greeks brought in to smash a strike in the Bingham County, Utah, copper mines. These nonunion strikebreakers were then trotted out as evidence that the unions were unrepresentative of the work force.

Immigrants permitted themselves to be used by employers because they expected to return home and most were unaware that the argument between labor and management had anything to do with them. Early labor historians often failed to recognize that after their initial reluctance to unionize, immigrants played a leading role in the unionization of America's work-force. Labor historian John R. Commons, writing in the midst of the new immigration, described the immigrants as "unfamiliar with the traditions and customs of [labor] organizations, unac-customed to the rules and control which it imposes, incapable of [unionizing] through their ignorance of the language, and more-over, forced by their poverty to work for low wages, and, by the lack of friends to work with docility and desperate energy for him who gives them a job." However, many Mediterranean im-migrants, unable to speak English and unfamiliar with Amer-ican customs, preferred to place their confidence in their own labor brokers, or *padrones,* to secure jobs for them on the construction sites of buildings, bridges, and roads.

Italian padrones operated in European cities as well as in the Italian enclaves of American cities. Humbert Nelli, a student of the Italian experience in Chicago, has explored the crucial role of the Italian padrone. According to Nelli, the padrone was the Italian immigrant's intermediary—"someone who spoke both languages, understood old-world traditions, and new-world business operations, and could get in touch with American employers who needed unskilled workers." While the padrone served a crucial function in the immigrant community, enough of these ethnic labor bosses made illegal profits at the expense of workers to give a bad name to the entire group. At times, the padrone charged workers first class transportation rates, though the employer had provided free passage. At other times, a contractor might pay the laborers' wages directly to the boss, who then paid workers whatever he wished, keeping the rest for himself. Some padrones accepted brokers' fees but never delivered the promised jobs. Yet, despite the risk of being duped, many unskilled ethnic workers relied on padrones to provide them with regular work. At the turn of the century, padrones controlled over 50 percent of New York City's Italian labor force. Not until the beginning of unionization in the construction industry, coupled with the labor shortages produced by World War I, did the power of the padrone diminish.

Greek immigrants, too, relied upon padrones and suffered the exploitation that so frequently resulted from dealing with these labor brokers. Among Greeks, the system was virtually a contemporary version of the indentured servant system popular in the late seventeenth and early eighteenth centuries. A Greek padrone, knowing shopkeepers in need of labor, wrote letters to relatives and friends in Greece telling them of the opportunities available to ambitious boys in America. Often the padrone offered to arrange for transportation and accommodations for a time after arrival. Greek male adolescents whose families agreed were sent to America and apprenticed to grocers, restaurant keepers, shopowners, or bootblacks for a period of three months to a year. Only then would the boy receive any salary—usually ten to twenty dollars per year. The peasant family had one less child at the table and often benefited from its son's earnings. The desire to live in America and the promise of advancement overshadowed harsh treatment and low wages; there was an inexhaustible supply of apprentices. American businessmen dealt with padrones because they could provide workers at a cost far below the market rate. If workers protested, the padrone could even provide strikebreakers for a fee. Leonidas G. Skliris, known as the "Czar of the Greeks," earned his notoriety for his ability to serve his clients regardless of the amount of coercion and extortion required.

The Chinese Six Companies, a benevolent association in San Francisco, performed labor brokerage services for immigrant Chinese without exploiting them. The Companies derived its name from the six regions of China where most emigrants to America came from. When a ship docked on the West Coast, representatives of the Six Companies boarded and offered the newcomers not only jobs but shelter, food, and other assistance. In return, immigrants paid dues to the Companies from their wages and were required to list on the Companies' books all loans and services for which they owed the organization. Should they return to China, members were required to first clear their account with the Companies. Few Chinese refused to join as there was no alternative source of assistance and protection for Chinese workers in the United States.

Recently, Gerald Rosenblum has argued that the new immigrants did not reject collective action completely, but that they were slow to organize and preferred a conservative brand of unionism to the more radical rejection of the American economic system. Most immigrants were strangers to American society; they had no prior acquaintance with the labor system they were entering and did not perceive themselves to be victimized by the new industrial order as many American-born workers did. They saw little purpose in protesting a divergence from an older, preindustrial order in the United States that they had never personally experienced and did not miss. However, they would eventually be drawn to unions by the prospect of higher wages and improved working conditions.

Studies of individual groups appear to confirm Rosenblum's hypothesis. The Slavic community has been traditionally regarded by labor historians as especially resistant to unionism because they accepted employment as scabs in mines and factories where workers were on strike. Also, Slavs appeared to see themselves as having little in common with non-Slavic workers. However, Victor Greene's study of Slavic labor organization in the anthracite coal districts of Pennsylvania suggests a modified perspective. According to Greene, the Slavs made decisions on issues such as labor organization within the context of their community. Once the comunity approved the strike as a device to hike income, it demanded conformity of its members. As early as 1887, Slavs supported collective action. Greene attributes the misconception of the Slavic perspective to the insensitivity of native-born union organizers who neglected immigrant fears of deportation or political repression such as many had witnessed in their native countries. Moreover, many Slavs at first perceived themselves to be "birds of passage," here only temporarily and therefore not in need of union membership.

Some new immigrant groups were more predisposed than others to collective action, and some unions were initially almost ethnically homogeneous. East European Jews, many of whom had previous experience in the shops and factories of their native countries, quickly embraced unionization in New York's largely Jewish garment industry and dominated the unions formed by garment workers. Even so, early labor organization went slowly.

In 1900, the United Brotherhood of Cloakmakers was formed. It was a small union, and by 1906 only 2,500 of the 42,500 cloakmakers were unionized. However, the inhuman conditions of labor and resistance of employers triggered greater militancy among both male and female workers. Garment workers were encouraged by the successful strikes of shirtwaistmakers in 1909 and cloakmakers in 1910. However, no single development galvanized workers more than the Triangle Shirtwaist fire of 1911.

The factory was a ten-story building. The fire started on the eighth floor and spread rapidly through the bolts of fabric to the various floors. The doors of the workrooms were locked from the outside, a practice followed by some employers to keep workers from leaving work early. The fire escapes were inadequate to support the fleeing occupants. One hundred fifty-four persons perished in the blaze, many of them young girls who did piecework in the shop. Newspaper reports repeated the harrowing details of how those trapped inside crowded onto window ledges and then threw themselves to the street, their clothing on fire:

The hair of some of the girls streamed up aflame as they leaped. Thud after thud sounded on the pavements . . . on both the Greene Street and Washington Place sides of the building there grew mounds of dead and dying. And the worst horror of all was that in this heap of the dead now and then there stirred a limb or sounded a moan. When fire chief Croker could make his way into these three floors he found . . . bodies burned to bare bones . . . skeletons bending over sewing machines.

The horror of the Triangle Shirtwaist fire stimulated labor militants. As a result, the International Ladies Garment Workers' Union and later the Amalgamated Clothing Workers of America, each of which had a largely Jewish, Italian, and Polish membership, developed into two of the strongest labor unions in the United States. David Dubinsky and Jacob Potofsky, respectively the leaders of these unions, became nationally known as fighters for the right of all workers to have strong, honest unions.

The millions of new immigrants who entered the American labor force between 1880 and 1921 did in part determine the pattern of labor union activity during the twentieth century. They were used by management to cross picket lines and break strikes in labor disputes. They held down the wage scale by initially accepting lower salaries than American workers. They undermined agitation by sometimes refusing to strike. But their sheer numerical strength ultimately made the new immigrants an asset to the labor organizers. The results of their eventual participation in collective action were higher wages, health benefits, pension plans, and other provisions that permitted workers in the United States to enjoy eventually a fairer share of the wealth their labor generated.

III

While union membership was the key to better wages and safer working conditions for millions of new immigrants, many newcomers pursued prosperity and prestige by leaving labor's ranks altogether. They became independent entepreneurs seeking the increased income and independent life-style of self-employment. Even in cases where the increase in real wages was minimal, the intangible benefits of being one's own boss in America attracted many newcomers. As in the case of all other new immigrant economic activity, cultural values, historic experience, and future expectations were as critical as marketplace conditions, if not more so, in determining the kind of business enterprises these new entrepreneurs would find attractive.

The new immigrant who was fired with ambition to succeed but hamstrung by limited capital traditionally took up the peddler's pack, or its urban counterpart, the pushcart. The pushcart was a large wooden cart on two wheels that could be pushed from block to block and neighborhood to neighborhood. The pushcart peddler, his cart loaded with fruits, vegetables, fish packed in ice, or dry goods, had no overhead and needed only enough capital to purchase his wares. Peddlers were popular with immigrant consumers. Often catering specifically to their own ethnic group, these outdoor merchants carried delicacies and goods reminiscent of the old country. They often spoke the old language and understood the old customs and mores. Also, pushcart peddlers sold food in small quantities for those with makeshift kitchens and limited funds. Profits were never great, but a pushcart peddler sometimes saved enough to open a small shop in the neighborhood where his customers lived.

Many Jewish immigrants had already been small merchants

on the streets of small towns and cities in Poland and Russia so the grip of the American pushcart fit naturally in their hands. Moreover, the pushcart removed Jews from under the hand of especially discriminatory non-Jewish employers. Religious Jews could arrange their business days to permit observance of holidays, attendance at religious services, or abstention from labor on Friday evening and Saturday. According to Charles Bernheimer, a contemporary writer, by 1905, New York City had almost one thousand Jewish "peddlers and keepers of stands, the number varying according to the season of the year." A day before the Sabbath, Hester Street, a center of New York's pushcart trade was alive with shouting vendors selling to housewives whatever they needed for the Sabbath. Everything from carp, to coffee, to candles was for sale in various quantities and at affordable prices. In the 1840s many of the "Yankee peddlers" who traveled the backroads of rural America, especially the south, were actually German Jews. Now Russian Jews, especially those who entered through the port of Baltimore, purchased backpacks or wagons and headed for the small towns of the south where the competition for business was far less than in northeastern cities.

Italians and Greeks also peddled. However, these groups found other jobs equally acceptable. Shoeshining was a popular entering wedge into the economy for Greeks and Italians. All one needed were strong arms and backs, a minimal knowledge of English, and a willingness to work seven-day weeks, including holidays from morning to night. In 1894, Italians constituted all but one of New York City's 474 foreign-born bootblacks.

The Greeks dominated the confectionery industry in the United States. Theodore Saloutos, in writing about Greek Americans, noted that some Greek entrepreneurs learned to make candies and cakes in Greece, "for the Greeks always have been known as a people with a sweet tooth." Once in the United States an individual could open a small shop in a Greek neighborhood and soon his kitchen would be supplying the needs of nearby coffeehouses, grocery stores, restaurants, and luncheonettes. Because Greeks celebrate religious and cultural occasions with feasts, the confectioner might cater the sweets at "wedding receptions, christenings, or the celebration of name days."

The experience of the pioneer Greek candy merchants who arrived even before 1880, as described by Saloutos, might well serve as an archetype of the new immigrant's entrance into the American world of free enterprise.

The pioneer confectioners were Eleutherios Pelalas of Sparta and Pangiotis Hatzideris of Smyrna, who established a lukum (sweet) shop shortly after their arrival in 1869. This partnership was terminated within a brief time; in 1877 Pelalas assumed the management of an American-owned establishment in Springfield, where he later opened a series of stores. Hatzideris, on the other hand, formed a partnership with another associate in New York, which handled more commercialized brands, such as "Turkish Delight" and "Greek Prince." Hatzideris eventually returned to Smyrna, but his partner continued the business under the name of Higgis Greek-American Confectionery Company, with plants in New York, Memphis, and Pittsburgh. The establishments of Pelalas and Hatzideris furnished employment for many of the first immigrants from Sparta, providing an opportunity to learn the skills of the trade.

Chicago became "the Acropolis of the Greek-American candy business," according to Saloutos. The Greek newspaper, *Hellinikos Astir,* reported in 1904 that "practically every busy corner in Chicago is occupied by a Greek candy store." It has been estimated that at one time, 70 percent of the Greek candy merchants in the United States were in Chicago and that Chicago money and training established candy stores throughout the South and West.

The immigrant's choice of occupation, while largely the product of group values and personal preferences, was also affected by competition from native Americans. Working on ladies' garments seemed unmanly to many native-born laborers, but not to Russian Jews and Italians. As a result these newcomers faced little native competition for jobs in a growing industry. Many Jews had already worked as tailors in the small towns of the Pale and the Italians appreciated work which could be done at home or in nearby factories where relatives could work side by side.

Asian immigrants also were quick to capitalize on the prejudices of other ethnic groups. Betty Lee Sung in *The Story of the Chinese in America* (1967) indicates that Chinese did not define such domestic tasks as cooking, ironing, and washing as strictly "women's work." Nor were male Chinese repelled by performing these jobs as were most American workers. Instead, the Chinese found laundering, especially in towns with many single men, could prove a lucrative trade. Only a scrubboard, some soap, an iron, and an ironing board were needed. Sung estimates that by 1880, more than 7,500 Chinese in San Francisco earned their livings in laundries. When the Chinese moved eastward, they continued to set up laundries, seeking out low-rent locations in those towns or cities in which they chose to settle. While few Chinese grew wealthy as launderers, owning their means of livelihood insulated them to a degree from Americans terrified by the "Yellow Peril."

The food industry was the lever by which many immigrants pried open the door of American opportunity. A food store might broaden its stock to cater to the preferences or ritual necessities of specific ethnic groups. Other stores achieved success by capturing an exclusive clientele. The strict Jewish dietary laws concerning meat, for example, drew many east European Jews into the meat and poultry business. It is estimated that in 1888, approximately half of New York City's 4,000 meat retailers and 300 wholesalers were Jewish. By 1900, 80 percent of the wholesale and 50 percent of the retail meat trade was in Jewish hands. Bakery products were also important to Jews, and Jewish bakeries swelled to number almost 500 across the city. By contrast, Greeks and Italians handled most of the fruit and vegetable trade.

As immigrants became more prosperous, ethnic restaurants opened. The restaurateurs, often immigrants themselves, knew the recipes that were popular with their particular group and the style of service that made the members of that group feel most comfortable. Some of the eateries, such as Mama Leone's (1906) specializing in Italian dishes, and Lüchow's (1882) a German restaurant, both in New York City, achieved national recognition for their cuisine.

Capital to begin any kind of business was scarce, and few immigrants were able to finance businesses after covering the cost of moving to America. So, some labored long hours, lived frugally, and hoarded the necessary funds. Others borrowed from relatives. However, neither savings nor personal loans were realistic options for immigrants supporting large families or lacking affluent friends or relatives. Few banks were willing to lend money to an immigrant whose only collateral were his hands, his back, and his nerve.

Thus, new immigrants formed self-help organizations to accumulate money. The Italians, the Chinese, and the Japanese each evolved mutual-assistance organizations to provide business capital. According to sociologist Ivan Light, the decisive community ties among the Japanese in America were those created by *ken* affiliations. The *kenjinkai,* or ken, were social organizations based on the provincial origins of Japanese immigrants. Most Japanese were eligible for membership in some ken organization. Fellow members, or *kenjin,* celebrated holidays together, enjoyed parties and picnics, and provided needed economic and social aid such as legal services and direct relief to the destitute. The kenjinkai founded employment agencies for members, and ken fellows tended to congregate in the same trades.

A crucial aspect of ken operation was a paternalism which made it a social obligation of an employer to enable a talented and loyal employee to open a business of his own; guild organizations regulated competition to prevent internal chaos. Japanese also had the *ko, tanomoshi* or *mujiri*—all names for rotating credit associations which assisted members in starting enterprises. As with kenjinkai, members were often from the same provinces.

The Cantonese *hui* and its variations were the rotating credit institutions most often used by Chinese to acquire business capital. The basic principle of the hui is useful in understanding all similar associations of this type. An individual needing a lump sum of money gathered a group of friends, each of whom agreed to pay a stipulated amount, perhaps $10, per month into a pool. In a hui of twelve members, the organizer himself received the first lump sum created, or $120. A month later, he held a feast in his home for the other contributors. At the feast, each member contributed another $10. A lottery decided which member (excluding the organizer) would get the total. Each member could get the lump sum only once and the lottery continued at subsequent feasts until every participant received his lump sum of $120. The organizer never contributed to the pool, but did provide twelve feasts costing $10 per feast. At the end of the twelfth feast, each member had spent $120 over the year and received one lump sum of $120 plus twelve feasts. The organizer of the hui had received the interest-free use of $120 when he needed it, ten of the twelve members had received an advance on their contributions, and all had enjoyed twelve fine meals.

The Chinese, like the Japanese, often associated with provincial neighbors in American cities. They, too, formed brotherhoods for benevolent and business purposes. In San Francisco, the Chinese Six Companies were later joined by other district associations and renamed the Chinese Consolidated Benevolent Association. There were also clan associations known by the last names of families. Thus, the Wong Association included all those in the city with the surname Wong. Everyone in these associations addressed each other as cousin, though they were not related as such in the Western sense. Surname associations tended to care for the social and benevolent services, while the district associations were involved in business operations such as the extension of loans for new businesses. The *tongs* (literally translated as "halls"), known in American lore for their fierce wars in the streets of Chinatowns, were originally fraternal organizations transplanted from China. However, in the streets of America, some tongs turned into violent gangs selling protection to brothels and gambling houses. Various tongs battled with each other for influence and territory, sidestepping control by American police and terrorizing Chinese communities. Tong wars did not cease until the 1930s when the function of the tongs was usurped. Disputants within the Chinese community were granted hearings before the Chinese Benevolent Association and members of genuine fraternal organizations substituted the name "lodge" or "association" for tong to indicate their desire to dissociate their group from the gangs of racketeers.

The southern Italians also organized themselves by old-world residential patterns. In Utica, New York historian John Briggs found a very active *Societa Calabria,* founded in 1903. These natives of Calabria joined together to foster "concord, brotherhood, education, instruction, work, [and] honesty." In large cities, these lodges kept their membership exclusive and were sometimes criticized by community leaders for encouraging divisiveness based on old-world rivalries. However, in smaller cities and towns the territorial exclusiveness was often compromised in the competition for dues-paying members from a limited pool of Italians. Members' dues financed social affairs and aided the sick and destitute. Rarely, however, did such societies finance individual entrepreneurial activity. Joseph Lopreato contends that, "cooperative ethnic activity" came hard to the Italians because the "vicissitudes of their history" have left Italians with trust only in family members. In his classic study of a town in southern Italy, Edward Banfield (*The Moral Basis of a Backward Society,* 1958) refers to this avoidance of cooperative behavior outside the nuclear family as "amoral familialism." Banfield contends that this "family-centered ethos" resulted from the poverty, isolation, and feudalism that persisted in southern Italy, perpetuating archaic patterns of social interaction. Upon arrival in the United States, many southern Italians found that such nonaltruistic behavior was an impediment to the voluntarism necessary for cooperative ventures and mutual assistance so profitably undertaken by other immigrant groups.

Most banks were hesitant to serve the needs of the new immigrants. Moreover, many of the newcomers avoided the austere offices and judgmental stares of native-born bankers. The result was the development of ethnic banks, willing to make small loans and prepared to send money overseas to relatives anxiously awaiting help. At times such banks were so informally arranged that transactions were conducted over the bar of the local tavern. Occasionally, one of those ethnic banks evolved into a major financial institution. Such was the experience of Amadeo Pietro Giannini's Bank of Italy in San Francisco. As Andrew Rolle and others have noted, Giannini became "the banker to a generation of immigrant fishermen, fruit peddlers, and small ranchers, and workmen."

Giannini, the son of a successful immigrant merchant, founded his bank to aid fellow Italians and to keep them from the teeth of loan sharks charging fantastic rates of interest. Giannini also hoped to teach Italian immigrants how to maneuver successfuly in the American economy. He spoke publicly about the virtues of interest-bearing savings accounts and pledged that he would loan any worker up to twenty-five dollars "with no better security than the callouses on the borrower's hands." Giannini's shrewd investments and faith in the small saver paid high dividends. After the San Francisco fire in 1906, he transacted business on the wharf, not waiting until a new building was prepared. By the time of his death in 1949, Giannini's bank, renamed the Bank of America, was the largest bank in the world.

I V

Most new immigrants did not throw themselves wholeheartedly into the pursuit of wealth; they were equally as interested in structuring their lives to protect family and religious customs brought from their native countries. However, few immigrants were content to remain impoverished and most made at least modest economic gains. It is this advancement from candy peddler to store owner, from delivery boy to launderer, from sewing

machine operator to tailor—rather than from rags to riches—
that has particularly intrigued historians and caused most of
them to define upward mobility occupationally.

In his now classic study of social mobility in Newburyport,
Massachusetts, in the nineteenth century (*Poverty and Progress,*
1964) historian Stephan Thernstrom described an "ideology of
mobility" that operated to provide Americans with "a scheme
for comprehending and accommodating themselves to a new
social and economic order." According to this mobility ideology, the United States had a uniquely fluid society, the defining
characteristic of which was its competitiveness. Each citizen who
competed, according to the ideal, was guaranteed that his social
status would be determined by his merit. The wealthy and
prestigious could remain so only as long as they performed well;
the talented born to lowly station could be certain to ascend
quickly to the riches and social position befitting their demonstrated worth. Failure to succeed in such a system could only be
interpreted as the product of an individual's inadequacy; most
certainly not the result of social injustice as was the case in the
Old World.

From early in the nineteenth century onward, the ideology
of success was popularized and restated so that all Americans
could comprehend it. Politicians, ministers, teachers, and journalists all reiterated the notion—especially when they addressed
the poor—that in an open society, there could be no obstacles
that an industrious man could not surmount. One newspaper,
the *Newburyport Herald,* reminded its readers that, "If Washington had whined away his time after the defeat on Long
Island, he would never have been the victor at Yorktown; but he
put himself to work to make up his losses." Such examples made
the point and suggested that initial failure did not preclude eventual success, a valuable means of forestalling disillusionment
and encouraging optimism among even the least affluent.

Success was most frequently defined as rising above the
level of manual labor. In urban factories or mills, the laborer
might become a foreman, clerk, manager, or even owner. How-

ever, increasingly, small business came to be viewed by Americans as the path to mobility. With a minimum of capital, the workman could become a businessman.

A second measure of success was more modest. Rather than a change in occupational level, success could be defined by the criterion of property ownership. Thus, it could be immaterial whether a man worked with his head or his hands, for himself or someone else. What mattered was whether a man owned the roof over his head or could purchase it with the money in his bank account.

By the end of the nineteenth century, the ideology of success was well ensconced in American mythology. The novels of Horatio Alger became manuals for the young. However, most immigrants arriving after 1880 had never been exposed to the ideology of success. Even more importantly, new immigrants brought with them their own definitions of success, or the good life, quite different from those set forth in America's mobility ideology.

Immigrants who arrived with the limited purpose of increasing their incomes, saving most of what they earned, and then returning home often stayed longer than they had planned and launched careers they had never intended. Therefore, historians have found occupational mobility rates useful in calculating one measure of newcomers' achievement in the American economy. Historians whose works have treated new immigrant groups such as Humbert Nelli (*Italians in Chicago,* 1970), Stephan Thernstrom (*The Other Bostonians,* 1973), Josef J. Barton (*Peasants and Strangers,* 1975), and Thomas Kessner (*The Golden Door,* 1977) have mapped occupational changes intragenerationally and intergenerationally within and among immigrant groups and sometimes between newcomers and the native born. However, disagreements often occur over the reasons why mobility rates vary from group to group.

The studies seem to concur that while the southern Italians did eventually achieve occupational upward mobility, their rate of upward mobility was somewhat sluggish compared to that of native-born blue-collar workers and other immigrant groups, especially the east European Jews. Some, such as historian Thomas Kessner, contend that southern Italian peasants suffered an initial disadvantage in the American economy because their agrarian skills and preferences for outdoor labor allowed them to do little more than wield pick and shovel on construction sites in America's industrial cities when they first arrived. However, historian John Briggs (*An Italian Passage,* 1978) points out that many of the Italian immigrants he studied had never been peasants at all but had had entrepreneurial experience in Italian towns. He suggests that indecision over whether or not their move to America was permanent, not a lack of urban skills, resulted in lower rates of upward mobility.

There is less disagreement about the east European Jews. Their rate of occupational mobility was indisputably the highest among the new immigrants. Many members of this group had learned trades or become entrepreneurs in Europe because they were denied land ownership and other economic opportunities. They valued their status as independent artisans and tradesmen because it freed them from the supervision of a potentially hostile Gentile boss, a sine qua non of survival in their countries of origin. Moreover, because the Jews were in flight from Russian pogroms, there was no doubt in most of their minds that they were in America to stay and should begin to focus their attention on their role in the American economy.

While mobility studies have been useful in assessing the agility of various immigrant groups on the occupational status ladder, such studies were not designed to deal with the broader, more subjective issue of success or whether immigrants found it possible to live the good life, as they defined it, in the United States. Occupational mobility and high incomes were often just part of more complex tableaux.

As James Henretta ("The Study of Social Mobility: Ideological Assumptions and Conceptual Bias," *Labor History,* 18, Spring 1977, 165–178) has observed, each immigrant group had its unique definition of success, which frequently included noneconomic criteria. Cultural and social priorities as well as historical experience shaped occupational choices and other economic decisions. Newcomers sought to carve out satisfactory niches in the economy that did not require abandonment of essential habits, customs, and values—all noneconomic but critical ingredients of the good life.

Among Greeks and southern Italians, education, job success, and even the acquisition of great wealth were not permitted to take precedence over the preservation of the family's integrity and the patterns of loyalty and support that the family engendered. To the southern Italian, work was something one did to acquire sufficient money to be comfortable and not for personal fulfillment or satisfaction. Those who expected anything more than a living from their jobs were often viewed by relatives and friends as self-indulgent and as an insult to the previous generation whose status they were striving to exceed.

Travelers from southeast Europe and the Mediterranean often ignored the pursuit of greater upward mobility in America because they were "birds of passage" and regarded their visits to the United States as work junkets rather than a permanent commitment to a new life. Males who came to work during the spring, summer, and fall wanted only to return to their families more prosperous than when they had left. Only when they finally decided to remain in America and send for their families did Greeks, Italians, Poles, and Slavs recast their career plans along lines that led to improved occupational status. Even, then, however, more traditional ethnic economic patterns persisted. Those who came from countries where land was the basis of all wealth often pursued property ownership more vigorously than occupational change, always preferring, according to sociologist Richard Gambino, "secure but gradual low-growth returns rather than the lucrative and faster but more risky possibilities of speculation."

By contrast, most east European Jews were not even initially "birds of passage." Those who arrived, especially after the Kishniev pogroms of 1903, intended to remain. For the orthodox, the good life consisted of being able to live and worship in a manner consistent with Mosaic law and religious tradition. Not all east European Jews were equally religious, but most were imbued with the Jewish cultural respect for intellectual pursuits. Rabbis, teachers, and others who worked with their minds instead of their hands were highly regarded within the Jewish community. Translated into secular occupations, Jews in America often preferred professional positions for their children—doctor, lawyer, professor—even to more lucrative business careers. American reformer and journalist, Jascob Riis, credited Jewish immigrants with recognizing that, beyond its intrinsic value, knowledge is power: "The poorest Hebrew knows—the poorer he is the better he knows it—that knowledge is power, and power is the means for getting on in this world that has spurned him so long, [knowledge] is what his soul yearns for. He lets no opportunity slip to obtain it." Moreover, unlike the Italians, east European Jews were encouraged to surpass their parents. Work was supposed to bring satisfaction and respect as well as a living. And the honor accorded an individual was seen to reflect on the entire family. Success thus did not estrange the child from the parents; it elevated the entire family's social position.

Though fewer studies have been done of the Chinese than other new immigrant groups, it appears from the limited evidence that the Chinese immigrant's notion of the good life, too, was more complex than the pursuit of either occupational advancement or the acquisition of property. According to historian Betty Lee Sung, emphasis was placed on "scholarship, official position, and an illustrious family." Like the east European Jews, the Chinese valued learning. A learned man regardless of occupation or income was the object of respect in the community. Official titles and a personal reputation for honor were important to Chinese immigrants. Like the Jews, the Chinese were also drawn to the learned professions when discrimination did not bar them from entering.

Family responsibilities were as important among the Chinese as among the Italians. Filial piety was the cardinal rule. And to the Chinese, the word family included more than just parents and siblings; it connoted a broader group of relatives, a kinship group or clan. The individual was expected to subordinate personal goals and purposes to those of the family. However, because the good life also included a respect for scholarship and rank, Chinese youth were urged toward higher education and the professions when the family's economic exigencies did not require more short-term and lucrative occupational plans such as entrepreneurship.

Clearly, immigrants arriving between 1880 and 1921 were more complicated in their economic behavior and aspirations than Horatio Alger's "Ragged Dick." The vast majority of new immigrants did indeed come to the United States for economic advancement. Some found it. Mary Antin's memoir explains that her father left Russia not knowing precisely what he would find in America but with "the confidence of a well-equipped soldier going into battle." He did not grow suddenly rich in America. When he sent for his family, "He was so far from rich that he was going to borrow every cent of the money for our third-class passage; but he had a business in view which he could carry on all the better for having the family with him. . . . United in America, there were ten chances of our getting to our feet again to one chance in our scattered aimless state." Others were not as fortunate. One Ukrainian miner who was prevented from returning home only by the outbreak of World War I, recalled, "But if the war didn't break out in 1914, I would have zipped right back where I came from after a year or two! Oh sure, positively. I was like a slave here; twelve, thirteen hours a day in the mines." Another east European recalled that his mother had been a peddler as well as his father, but that both parents together could only "accumulate a little bit to enable them to support the family."

Occupational mobility statistics, then, indicate the slot immigrants held in America's economy and how it changed over time. But from the immigrant's perspective, success or personal satisfaction often transcended the color of his collar—white or blue—and even the size of his bank account. The good life often depended upon the newcomer reconciling his noneconomic values, traditions, and priorities with the material wealth he hoped to accumulate in the United States. Not all those who made the journey found satisfaction as well as wealth and position. Often their odyssey led them farther away from their past than they cared to go.

Contemporary novels in the immigrants' native language often placed the quest for economic advancement within the context of the larger issue of assimilation. How American did the immigrants become? What were the benefits and costs of Americanization? Nowhere is the dilemma more starkly recreated than in *The Rise of David Levinsky* (1917) by Yiddish novelist and journalist Abraham Cahan. Cahan's novel traces the odyssey of a Russian Jewish immigrant who compromises his religious values and sacrifices his passion for scholarship all for material success. Early in the novel, a young David laments that becoming "Americanized" undermined his daily religious practices. "The very clothes I wore and the very food I ate," David testified, "had a fatal effect on my religious habits." Much later in life, a weary Levinsky muses that "David, the poor lad swinging over a Talmud volume at the Preacher's Synagogue, seems to have more in common with my inner identity than David Levinsky, the well-known cloak-manufacturer."

Cahan's words touched a chord deep in the hearts of many immigrants who were, like David Levinsky, confronting the transformation of immigrant to American.

THE HUDDLED MASSES

An Essay in Photographs

by Alan M. Kraut and Sarah Larson

I / EUROPE

YIVO INSTITUTE FOR JEWISH RESEARCH

Jewish *fusgeyers* (Yiddish: travelers on foot) emigrating from Kovno, Lithuania with their belongings on their backs.

(Top) Travelers of many economic classes gather near the docks outside of the Hall of the Hamburg-Amerika shipping line, c. 1900.

(Bottom) Beneath an inscription that reads, "My field is the World," emigrants queue up to secure passage on a Hamburg-Amerika steamer, c. 1900.

On the deck of the S.S. Patricia in 1902, trans-Atlantic immigrants meet to chat, court, and play in the shadow of an open hatch.

The Statue of Liberty went unnoticed by many immigrants who were busy collecting belongings and children as their ships docked in New York Harbor. Others mistook it for the tomb of Columbus.

LIBRARY OF CONGRESS

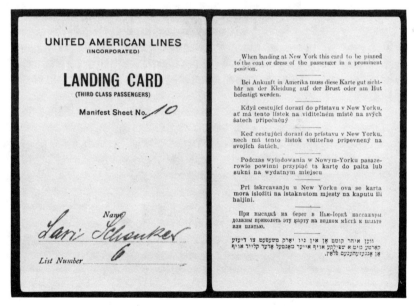

MS. HASSA F. SCHANKER

(Top) Immigration reception depot at Ellis Island.

(Bottom) Landing card of Lari Schanker from Russia, who arrived in America neatly tagged with all other third-class passengers.

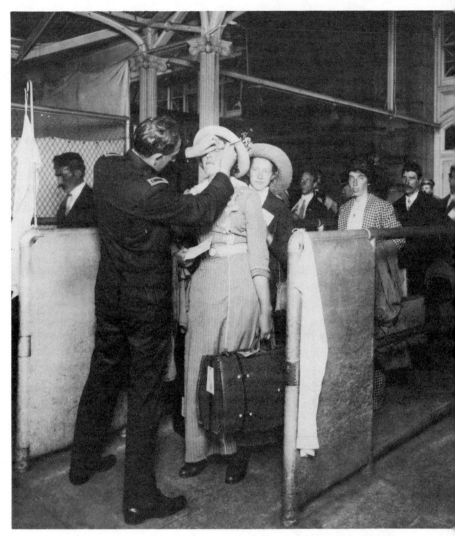

Checking for highly contagious trachoma, an official pries up a woman's eyelid with a buttonhook normally used for fastening gloves. Those with the illness were detained for treatment. The hook was not sterilized between inspections but merely wiped on the towel draped over the railing.

(Top) Health inspection of oriental immigrants at the Angel Island depot off the California coast.

(Bottom) After 1882, immigrants suspected of being "mentally defective" were subjected to the intelligence tests; failure meant deportation. Posted on the rear wall are the photographs of European heads of state, national flags, and playing cards, probably used in questioning.

On Ellis Island for Christmas, these somewhat bemused newcomers were gathered before a Christmas tree to be issued an apple and formally photographed, c. 1900.

(Top) In an attempt to protect Ellis Island immigrants from dishonest money exchangers, the American Express Company was given sole concession in 1905.

(Bottom) With their bundles and string-tied boxes, immigrants gaze across New York Harbor from the Ellis Island pier.

Pushcart peddlers, canny shoppers, and idle strollers leave little room for the horse-drawn wagons on one of New York's Lower East Side's many narrow streets, c. 1910.

The average seven story dumbbell tenement could house as many as 150 people and a shop on the ground floor; in warm weather tenants and merchants spilled out onto the front steps and sidewalk, c. 1900.

As American cities burgeoned, some immigrant families could only find affordable living quarters in alley shanties, c. 1900.

**Ironically, the tenement inspectors sent out by urban reform-
ers to protect the poor from exploitative landlords were hated
by the immigrants, who feared eviction on the basis of over-
crowding.**

U.S. NATIONAL ARCHIVES

As the newcomers scattered across the country, they put their hands to any work they could find, such as this Polish family who labored on the Bottomley berry farm near Rock Creek, Maryland from 4:00 a.m. to sunset, July 7, 1909.

Nine-year-old Johnnie, who was brought from Baltimore to shuck oysters in Dunbar, Louisiana, is closely watched by his padrone, March 2, 1911.

Some newcomers made their way in America by catering to the unique tastes and preferences of their own ethnic group, such as this Italian pasta maker, c. 1910.

Joseph Severio, an eleven year old peanut vendor in Wilmington, Delaware, worked six hours a day at his curbside pushcart, May 21, 1910.

Most of the employees in the spinning room of the Cornell Mill in Fall River, Massachusetts were children, January 11, 1912.

(Top) Using a skill they brought from Italy, the Malestestra family makes artificial flowers in New York, averaging ten to twelve gross a day at six cents a gross, 1908.

(Bottom) In sweatshops such as those in the New York City garment district, immigrants established a comraderie that overcame differences of language and culture, 1914.

As more immigrants realized that their stay in America would be permanent, the fledgling labor movement took on a multiethnic flavor.

Even as they protested working conditions, these striking immigrant clothing makers tried to look as American as their native-born customers.

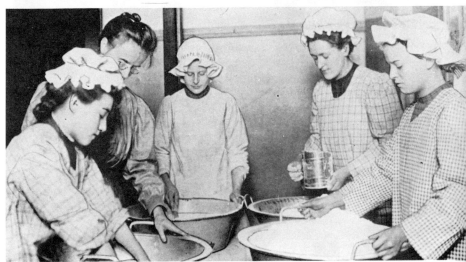

(Top) Anxious to help newcomers become self-supporting, reformers established free classes that were often taught at night, c. 1910.

(Bottom) Reformers also taught immigrant women how to make a good American home, to maintain middle-class standards of hygiene, and cook American food, c. 1910.

(Top) A class of immigrant mothers learning English, c. 1910.

(Bottom) Coming full circle, eastern and southern European immigrants perform the maypole dance in New York City's Central Park, a rite of spring imported by English immigrants almost three centuries earlier, May 1, 1913.

T. Kartman of Samara, Russia as he appeared in his home town, 1918, and as he appeared twelve years later in Brooklyn, New York.

Most immigrants made their own choices as to how rapidly and to what degree they would take on the trappings of American culture.

The priest blessing holiday breads baked in the new land exemplifies how organized religion served as a familiar focus for many immigrants struggling to adapt to America, Easter, c. 1920.

For immigrants living far from the large cities, such as most Mexican immigrants of the nineteenth century, retention of old habits and values was not difficult.

(Top) In urban neighborhoods, immigrants of the same national group often formed clubs, such as this Slavic dance society, in a deliberate attempt to preserve ethnic customs, c. 1920.

(Bottom) No matter how assimilated the immigrant, inherited ethnic customs assumed great significance at rites of passage such as birth, marriage, and death, as suggested by this Chinese funeral procession, c. 1910.

The Ku Klux Klan protested the "mongrelization" of American society, c. 1920.

THE AMERICANESE WALL, AS CONGRESSMAN
BURNETT WOULD BUILD IT.

UNCLE SAM: You're welcome in — if you can climb it!

Nativists argued that "undesirable" foreigners could be weeded out by
administering a literacy test at all immigration depots.

THE ONLY WAY TO HANDLE IT.

Immigration restriction based upon a quota system was widely applauded around the country, as this editorial cartoon suggests, c. 1921.

MR. & MRS. HARRY KRAUT

Restrictionists won only a Pyrrhic victory in 1921; over twenty-three million immigrants had entered the country since 1880 and would unalterably change the nature of American society and culture.

FOUR

Assimilation: Newcomer and Nation Transformed

For many immigrants, the first reaction to America was a tremendous sense of isolation. They were greenhorns, uninitiated in the ways of their new country, unable even to speak the language. They were harassed and ridiculed by older immigrants and native Americans for not knowing how to behave appropriately in their new home. Even compared with members of their own immigrant group, newcomers were nervous misfits with odd clothing and hairstyles unsuitably reminiscent of the old country. Often, newcomers were pressured most heavily by members of their own group to quickly become Americanized and not be embarrassingly different. The newcomers, meanwhile, felt awkward and were often shocked by the changes that life in America had already wrought on earlier arrivals. One Jewish immigrant recalled his first days in America: "I felt as if on coals. No word could I think of but 'greenhorn.'" On the streets he was startled by the appearance of young Jewish men and women. "The girls had painted cheeks and greased netted hair with hidden pins. As if that weren't enough, they also flashed golden teeth. They seemed faded and withered. The males with stiff hats tipped over their foreheads and their plastered locks, gave off an aroma of vulgar, youthful virility." His culture shock was typical of that experienced by many new arrivals. So it became essential for each immigrant to rapidly figure out what it meant to be an American and to decide which changes were worthwhile and which individual group customs and values were too important to relinquish.

Books of advice to new immigrants about techniques of assimilation proliferated in the late nineteenth century. Some were published by Americans hoping to impose their own design on immigrant behavior. Others were the legacy of earlier settlers. One of the latter, written in Yiddish and published in Russia in 1891, advised readers to,

Forget your past, your customs and your ideals. Select a goal and pursue it with all your might. No matter what happens to you, hold on. You will experience a bad time but sooner or later you will achieve your goal. . . .

The new immigrant was being encouraged to barter his past for a more satisfying future. However, for most new immigrants it was not a casual exchange. Historians such as Philip Taylor (*The Distant Magnet,* 1971) have rejected older depictions of assimilation as a smooth, almost mechanical process of one group's absorption by another. Instead, he contends that assimilation for the new immigrants ". . . was a series of conflicts between competing influences from the wider American society battling with the entrenched leadership of heads of families or of ethnic institutions." Though some groups and individuals assimilated more quickly and thoroughly than others, the weight of evidence tips the scales toward Taylor's contention.

New immigrants did not undergo their metamorphosis passively. Each newcomer made choices among a limited number of options that would shape his relationship to his new country and determine the rate and extent of assimilation. The immigrants did not make their choices in a vacuum, of course. They received assistance and advice, frequently unsolicited, from many sources with varied agendas. Benevolent aid societies, some operated by American charities and others run by members of their own ethnic groups, were quick to extend newcomers a helping hand. Public schools not only taught immigrant children the 3 Rs but assumed responsibility for socializing children and, indirectly, their parents, in the ways of American society. Even urban politicians, primarily concerned with acquiring the loyalty of new voters, became conduits for assistance and advice.

Various new immigrant groups, with their unique languages and cultural traditions, differed from one another and from the native born, or core society, as to what constituted an acceptable level of assimilation. Conformity required compromise, but how could sacred values and traditions be cast by the wayside? For all immigrants, Americanization was a struggle to reconcile the ways of the Old World with life in the New.

I

The earliest casualty in the adjustment process was an immigrant's native language. Many an immigrant was given a new identity by an Immigration Service Officer who couldn't understand or spell his name. Many others jettisoned family names ending in "a," "o," "ski," "sky," or "wicz." Names difficult for American tongues often became barriers to employment and acceptance, and stigmatized the foreign born. Thus, Irving Abramowitz became Irwin Abbot "for business reasons" and Pietro Minotti was dubbed Peter Minor.

It was necessary to speak English to get on a streetcar, ask directions, buy food, and obtain a job. Mastery of English would enable the recent arrivals to mingle easily with the native-born and earlier immigrants. Italians, Poles, and east European Jews often learned English as their neighbors spoke it. Their speech echoed not only their mother tongue but the regional cadences and inflections common to native speakers in Charleston, New Orleans, Boston, or New York. Often, immigrants spoke a hodgepodge of their native language and English. Richard Gambino (*Blood of My Blood,* 1974) recalls hearing his Italian immigrant neighbors call an automobile a "carra," a store a "storo," a bar a "barra," a job a "giobba," and a toilet a "baccausa" (because early tenements had been served by back or outhouses.)

English, however, was only to be a tool for advancement; settlers deplored the complete abandonment of their native tongues and were upset when their children quickly forgot the language of the old country. According to linguist Joshua Fishman (*Language Loyalty in the United States,* 1966), "language loyalty and language maintenance became curious goals for many immigrants."

One Italian newspaper editor wrote in 1903 that "in the civilization of the Italian language . . . [were] thousands of secrets for our future in America." Another, writing in the same period in Utica, New York, titled an editorial on the subject, "A Duty of the Heads of Families." He defined it as the duty of all Italian parents to be certain that their children learn Italian, because "although born here they are Italians and have, thus, the right to know the language of their homeland." He quickly added that since the children learned English at school, there could be little harm in a father insisting that Italian be spoken exclusively in the home.

But, the more immigrant parents insisted that Yiddish, Italian, or Polish be spoken in homes, the more their children rebelled. As they grew to adulthood, the children of the immigrants realized that a fluent command of the language was a critical ingredient of socioeconomic mobility. English, spoken as if by a native-born American, was a prerequisite for gaining entrance to a prestigious college, getting a high-salaried job, meeting the right people, including the right girl or boy, and becoming an authentic American. Occasionally, those of the second generation became hypersensitive, ashamed of the ethnic identity, so clearly revealed in their parents' accents.

An indignant son wrote a letter to Abraham Cahan, the editor of *The Forward,* a Yiddish language newspaper, to complain of his father's public use of Yiddish, the language shared by most east European Jews. The son, a big success in America, had taken his father shopping in a fashionable Fifth Avenue shop and became embarassed to the point of anger when his father spoke Yiddish to a clerk whom he suspected of being Jewish. Cahan scolded the young man for berating his father, but also lectured the father on the importance of speaking English in America. Such were the pains inflicted by one generation upon another as both struggled to cope with the dilemma of assimilation. Cahan, himself an immigrant from Russia, encouraged newcomers to write letters which he published in the *Forward's* "Bintel Brief" ("Bundle of Letters") column, which he inaugurated in 1906. Cahan believed that the immigrants should share with each other their problems and questions about America. He, Cahan, would try to offer advice which would help the newcomers to adjust to their new life without sacrificing their dignity or their Jewish heritage.

New immigrants were limited to the least expensive housing available and often chose, within these constraints, to live in close proximity to those who had emigrated from the same town or village as themselves. Many large and midsized cities had little Italies, Chinatowns, and enclaves of Polish, Russian, and Ukrainian immigrants. On New York City's Lower East Side, members of particular immigrant groups even dominated specific tenement buildings. In their neighborhood, new immigrants and their children could envelop themselves in a sort of cocoon, almost completely avoiding contact with other groups and the core society. Often, regional distinctions as well as national differences kept immigrants apart from each other, even determining housing patterns on an urban block or in a neighborhood. Old world loyalties linked those who had been neighbors before emigrating, while strangers viewed each other with time-honored wariness. In the streets of America, Athenians still considered Spartans ignorant, slow, and pugnacious, while Spartans found the Athenians as effete and decadent as they had seemed in Greece. Northern Italians who removed to America brought with them their contempt for *Il Mezzogiorno,* while the distinctive dialects and attitudes of Neapolitans, Calabrians, and Genoese were so divisive, southerners had little more than their mutual distrust of the Sicilians in common. Jews from Galicia, a province of Austria, and those from Lithuania or neighboring regions shunned each other. *Galitzianers* regarded themselves as generally better educated and more secular than their less enlightened, often more orthodox coreligionists from farther east. However, the Lithuanians, or *Litvaks,* dismissed Galitzianers as pedants, a dry humorless lot who were hardly as shrewd or worldly wise as Litvaks for all the westerners' pretensions of superiority. Surrounded by familiar faces, immigrants could continue to speak their native language, eat familiar foods, and conduct family and religious lives in traditional fashion. Thus, the immigrant could use his neighborhood to resist the pressure to assimilate that he encountered each day in other parts of the city.

At times, however, the ethnic neighborhood could be as much help as a hindrance to assimilation. Such enclaves could function as incubators, providing the new immigrants and their children with a supportive environment until they were sufficiently prepared and confident to venture forth and mingle with the native-born and members of other immigrant groups.

Ethnic neighborhoods developed, then, by choice rather than compulsion. Immigrants chose to live close to their work and among others who shared their culture and lifestyle. According to historian Caroline Golab (*Immigrant Destinations,* 1977), "If the conditions of work remained favorable long enough to keep the newcomers rooted to their piece of city-space, the ethnic neighborhood and community could be formed, complete with its unique industrial and occupational structures." In New York, the garment factories where most Jews and Italians worked were within walking distance from Lower East Side tenements. In Golab's study of Philadelphia, she discovered that, "Jews and Italians settled in central parts of the city next to the major wholesale and retail markets that employed them in large numbers." However, the factories in which most of Philadelphia's Poles worked utilized the latest in industrial technology and required ample room for plant and transportation facilities. They were located in the newer or less settled areas of the city—Nicetown, Port Richmond, Bridesburg, southwest Philadelphia, and northwest Philadelphia—surrounded by the homes of their workers.

In most cities, no single ethnic group resided exclusively in a neighborhood. Usually three or four groups shared a corner of the city, but each group would be more concentrated on particular streets or even specific buildings. In Philadelphia's areas of high Polish concentration, Poles occupied most of the houses on particular streets, block after block. Similarly, on New York's Lower East Side, Jews and Italians shared the neighborhood, but each group held domain over particular blocks. Thus, different groups could live in close geographical proximity, and yet be socially isolated. This provincialism was mirrored within each ethnic enclave by residential patterns that echoed provincial and village configurations in the Old World. In Italian communities, families who were Sicilian, Calabrian, or Neapolitan—often from the same village in these provinces—again took up residence near one another in an American city.

Tucked within their ethnic communities, immigrants took refuge from the strangeness of American society. In his neighborhood, the immigrant found those who understood his native tongue and, perhaps, even his local dialect. There he could purchase familiar foods, prepared in traditional fashion, from merchants who might even haggle over the price or sell the merchandise in amounts small enough to fit every budget. In the neighborhood of an American city, an immigrant might find that group taboos and traditional codes of personal behavior derived from old-world experiences and wisdom all continued to have relevance. Richard Gambino recalls that after a fight he had with a childhood playmate, his Italian-born grandmother and the mother of the other young pugilist confronted each other and with a combination of body language and *passatella* (ritualized oratory) battled for their respective family's honor on a street in Red Hook, Brooklyn. No mere trans-Atlantic voyage could make superfluous proper decorum as determined by time-honored custom.

Neighborhoods changed character as different immigrant groups deserted them and moved on to better housing in less congested parts of the city. Newcomers then crowded into the empty buildings, bringing with them their own unique customs and culture. This process of change often took several generations. Moreover, even when economic prosperity permitted geographic mobility within the city, emmigrants returned periodically to "the old neighborhood." In New York, Chicago, and Philadelphia, immigrants followed expanding subway and bus lines into new neighborhoods. The subway offered not only an escape route, but a ride back home. Some returned daily, commuting from their new home to their old job. Others came just on weekends to visit friends and relatives, to shop, and to eat. In her description of Chinese communities in the United States (*Mountain of Gold,* 1967), Betty Lee Sung contends that Chinese cuisine preserved "Chinatowns" even after improved economic conditions had permitted some families to move away. Those families continued to serve traditional Chinese dishes in their homes, and the basic ingredients could only be purchased in Chinatown, "for where else can one buy soy sauce, bean curd, dried mushrooms, snow peas, and bamboo shoots?"

Though they walked the same streets, most immigrants had few contacts with members of other groups and even less with native-born Americans. Residential patterns encouraged this neighborhood provincialism. Only on the job, or while taking an English language course in the evening at a local public school, might immigrants encounter others not of their own kind. Perhaps employers or teachers would be native-born. Often, though, employers and teachers were merely those of one's own group who had arrived earlier and prospered. From the perspective of an immigrant, whether a resident of Chinatown, Little Sicily, or Little Warsaw, America was a patchwork of urban villages, perplexing to all who encountered it.

The nucleus of the ethnic neighborhood for the immigrant was frequently the house of worship. For most immigrants, the traditions, rituals, and sacred objects of their religions were important articles of cultural baggage brought from their native lands. Religious fealty, however, was often intertwined with regional and national identities. A distinctive feature of the new immigration was the multiplicity of diverse Catholic groups that joined the already heterogeneous American Catholic community. Sometimes these groups worshipped together, common faith transcending their differences. However, more often, their differences were obstacles to cohesion. Each group preferred its own clergy, who could conduct worship and serve congregants in the familiar patterns of their native communities. In neighborhoods where immigrant Catholics of different ethnic groups resided, newcomers felt most at home worshipping in their own churches.

Language differences were obvious and irritating to many congregants. Both Irish and French Canadians were Roman Catholics. However, in the New England parishes where Irish priests delivered their sermons in English, French-speaking Canadians were ill at ease; they viewed the insistence upon English as an attempt by Irish clergymen at Americanization, undermining their French heritage. Irish parishioners often treated newcomers speaking a foreign tongue as suspicious interlopers with designs on the church.

More than language, contrasting traditions and unique styles of worship accented national distinctions among Catholics. According to Helen Znaniecki Lopata (*Polish Americans,* 1976), "Polish peasants, particularly during the decades of heavy migration, combined a Polish version of Catholicism with pagan and magical beliefs in animated natural objects and spirits." A Polish immigrant far from his familiar church building and sacred objects, in need of spiritual comfort but repelled by the formalism of the Irish-dominated American Catholic Church, might turn to pagan superstitions acquired in his home village, cherishing amulets that had no place in Catholic iconography. He might sprinkle the floors of a newly acquired apartment with salt or coins before moving in to ensure his family's prosperity in their abode. Charms to ward off illness, assure fertility, or attract a particular member of the opposite sex were sometimes used in tandem with lighting candles in church or praying, rosary beads in hand.

Historians Josef Barton and Rudolph Vecoli have published essays that demonstrate how folk religion and community life deeply colored the Catholicism of Czech and Italian Catholic immigrants. The contadini described by Vecoli, for example, subscribed to a system of *clientelismo*. While God was a "lofty, distant figure," a local saint, as a "friend of God," could be a poor peasant's intermediary. Therefore, Italians prayed directly to particular saints—Santa Lucia, San Gennaro, San Michele, and others. Each saint had special jurisdiction over illness, business, or other particular fields of endeavor. In Italy the high point of a peasant's year was the celebration, or festa, in honor of the saint who looked after the town. The statue of the saint was carried through the town as part of a long and colorful procession complete with brass bands and weeping women.

These vibrant religious festivities were not immediately abandoned when villagers left for the New World. In the Little Italies of urban America, immigrants celebrated the patron saints of their native villages with the same parades, bands, and delicacies that they enjoyed in Italy. Such goings-on were frequently deplored by American Catholics who watched the religious processions clanging through the streets of Italian neighborhoods. To non-Italian Catholics these festivities seemed little more than pre-Christian pagan rites. Over time and several generations, these festas and other such customs were usually modified or abandoned by Italians hoping to blend in with other more assimilated, non-Italian Catholics. However, in some Italian neighborhoods, such as New York's Little Italy, festas in honor of St. Anthony and St. Gennaro continue to be celebrated with traditional enthusiasm.

Dissimilarities among Catholic immigrants significantly reduced the quality and quantity of emotional and material support rendered newcomers by the Church. Irish and German churchmen who had arrived earlier or were native-born looked unsympathetically upon ethnic parishes, embarrassed by newcomers' eclectic styles of Catholicism and apprehensive that ethnic rivalries might fracture the Church or, worse, dilute their own influence within it. Therefore, Church assistance was often contingent upon Americanization, a condition unsatisfactory to most immigrants, who preferred whenever possible to build and direct their own parish churches, parochial schools, and hospitals. Immigrants hoped to simultaneously preserve their peculiar version of Catholicism and their group's identity. Caroline Golab (*Immigrant Destinations*, 1977) observes that in Philadelphia, ''Poles preferred to build their own churches because they could not conceive of a church organization containing no Poles but only Irishmen and Germans.'' The Italians of Buffalo, New York, reports Virginia Yans-McLaughlin, viewed the Church as ''an Irish-American institution'' and therefore, ''remained either nominal Roman Catholics or without Church ties of any kind,'' until they could afford their own churches and priests. In Buffalo, the immigrants ''generally avoided the parochial schoods'' for similar reasons, though some parents found the Irish brand of Catholic education a lesser evil than Protestant flavored public education.

The oldest fissure in Catholicism had occurred in 1054 A.D., resulting in the complete separation between the Roman Catholic and Greek Orthodox Churches. In the United States, Greek immigrants clung to their own church, the priests clearly distinguished by their full beards, tall hats, and flowing robes. Whenever a *kinotis* (community) became sufficiently large and affluent it imported a priest from Greece and built a church, hoping to resist assimilation of its members by the more highly organized and affluent Roman Catholic Church.

Despite internecine discord, new immigrants clung to their religions, while adjusting the style of their religious practices to reflect their experience in America. Second-generation Greek immigrants worshipped in chapels that were bland replicas of the elaborate, ornate churches of their homeland. East European Jews, who had been orthodox in their native Russia or Poland, shaved their beards and sat next to their wives and daughters in the "conservative" synagogues they now preferred rather than the orthodox houses of worship where women were mostly secluded in balconies or behind curtains. Others who rarely attended services in their villages now became members of churches or synagogues to maintain close contact with those from home and to draw spiritual strength with which to confront the adversities of immigrant life. On New York City's Lower East Side, rabbis were known by the village in Russia or Poland from which they had emigrated and were sought out by former neighbors for advice.

Statistics on changes in religious practice are notoriously unreliable. However, a consensus among sociologists suggests that the religious lives of second and third generation new immigrants were generally less conventionally pious than the lives of most first generation new immigrants. As the children of the immigrants rebelled against their parents' piety which seemed old-fashioned and stifling, they frequently expressed their rebellion by shunning traditional religious expressions. Others, merely hoping to embrace America more quickly, readily abandoned religious customs and rituals which conflicted with the economic or social demands of American life. Many second generation east European Jews worked on Saturday, which was their Sabbath but a regular business day for their Gentile neighbors and employers.

Despite the fears of priests and rabbis, there was never a rush of second generation Catholic or Jewish immigrants to Protestant churches as a means to assimilation—not that there was no proselytizing. Many Protestant groups did invade immigrant enclaves with honed conversion techniques. Tract societies updated their publications to address a new generation of foreign-born readers and the Sunday School movement sought to make their weekly classes in Christianity appealing to the urban poor. By the turn of the century, Chicago Protestants were supporting over 120 Sunday schools in the slums. Also, itinerant evangelists such as Dwight L. Moody, financed by urban businessmen like John Wanamaker and William E. Dodge, conducted huge revival meetings aimed at newcomers in Brooklyn, Chicago, New York, and Philadelphia. The missionary movement, though less colorful than urban revivalism, was no less industrious. In 1883, the American Home Missionary Society, a Congregationalist agency, allocated a major share of its budget to work among the immigrants. The Congregationalists also established a $200,000 fund drive for the building of mission houses and churches in urban neighborhoods. Other denominations launched similar programs. The Baptist Home Missionary Society courted immigrant converts who would then be willing to convert others. A Polish Catholic convert, Joseph Antoshevski, conducted missionary work among Detroit's Poles in the late 1880s. Businessmen, as much concerned with preserving social peace as improving the moral order, encouraged missionary efforts with their dollars. Often they created nondenominational city missions. In Chicago, meatpacker Joseph F. Armour and his brother, Philip D. Armour, raised a $100,000 endowment for The Armour Mission, which opened in late 1886, only months after the Haymarket Riot had raised the specter of immigrant radicalism.

Well-financed by philanthropists or marginally supported with the loose change of sidewalk contributors, urban missionary work and evangelism won few converts among the immigrants. Discouraged by his lack of success with the newcomers in New York, Dwight Moody confessed, "The city is no place for me. . . . If it was not for the work I am called to do, I would never show my head in this city or any other again." Those immigrants who converted often did so before marriage to a Protestant who would not leave his or her own faith. Many Protestant clergymen conceded the strength of the immigrants' religiosity, especially that of Roman Catholics and orthodox Jews, and even found it reassuring. Protestant churchman Samuel Lane Loomis was content that Catholicism's influence was "doubtless conservative" and that as religions went it was "far better than none." That most Americanized immigrants retained their original faith, with many of the old-world customs and traditions, is testimony to the primacy of religion among newcomers and its resilience in the face of Protestantism's urban crusade.

The unfamiliar values, customs, and lifestyles that the new immigrants encountered each day in America often followed them home at night, gradually affecting their households and family relationships. Traditional clothing was quickly abandoned, especially by young women anxious to appear as attractive and stylish as their American sisters. For some groups, such as the orthodox Jews, changes in dress conflicted with religious law. Married women were required to wear a *sheitel* or wig publicly as a sign of modesty. Yet, many young wives changed their fashion to conform to the American style that their husbands found alluring. In 1902, Hutchins Hapgood observed,

If she is young when she comes to America, she soon lays aside her wig, and sometimes assumes the rakish American hat, (and) prides herself on her bad English. . . .

Shedding their wigs was for women, as shaving their beards was for men, an outward concession to America.

Women changed more than their appearance in America. Free public schools encouraged many new immigrant parents to allow their daughters at least an elementary school education. Compulsory attendance laws after 1918 persuaded the hesitant. Young women too old for school usually acquired their knowledge of American ways informally from co-workers. Many took evening classes to improve their English and learn American housekeeping.

One lesson women learned quickly was that in America

marriages were not prearranged by parents. In traditional societies, marriages were the products of family agreements, sometimes with the assistance of a marriage broker who was a member of the community and was hired by one or both families to make a match. With a favorable match, a family gained prestige or wealth through its new tie to a family of equal or greater reputation and resources. The happiness of the bride and groom was a lesser consideration and marriage for love alone was unthinkable—indicating an abdication of parental responsibility or the absence of filial respect. In Greece, a dowry was paid to the groom by the bride's family. Fathers and brothers labored hard to secure money for dowries lest the family be dishonored by unmarriageable daughters. A dutiful brother often postponed his own marriage until his sisters had dowries sufficient to attract husbands. During the height of emigration from Greece, marriages were frequently arranged across the sea with a system of "picture brides." These young ladies, betrothed by mail to men already in America, often came from the same village as their prospective mates and knew their families well. After the arrangement was struck, the bride would be sent to America by herself to meet and marry the man to whom she was promised. Few unengaged Greek women emigrated on their own, but those who did and later married in America spared their families the burden of the dowry. Among east European Jews, village *shadkans* or matchmakers often brought the "lucky" boy and girl together. After the marriage, the male ruled the household, while his wife managed it; there was little egalitarianism in such homes. Husband and wife had been socialized since childhood to fit these roles, and their "acceptable behavior" bore little resemblance to that in American marriages even during the rigid Victorian era. Increasingly, immigrant women from societies where marriages were prearranged demanded to choose their own mates on the basis of romantic love, an option that males were equally anxious to exercise.

As new immigrants modified their marriage patterns, they found that traditional child-rearing patterns were likewise altered. Italian, Greek, Slavic, and Oriental households were traditionally parent-centered. Age implied wisdom and the young were expected to show appropriate deference. Jewish households were more "child-centered," and parents tended to be more indulgent toward offspring than in other ethnic households. In general, however, new immigrant families resisted the comparative permissiveness of American family life as long as possible. Until the family achieved economic security, which frequently did not occur until the second or third generation, children were expected to perform tasks as if they were little adults. Childishness and play were often put aside by immigrant children at a much earlier age than by American children.

Still, child-rearing practices differed considerably among new immigrant groups. Greek, Slavic, and Italian children were permitted to spend more time learning from their peers than Jewish, Chinese, or Japanese children, who were closely supervised by parents. Oriental, Mexican, and Slavic boys were taught that manliness involved veiling their emotions, while Italian and Jewish boys were encouraged to express their feelings; even tears were permissible in certain contexts. These characteristics of child rearing, while modified somewhat by American schools and social workers, nevertheless proved remarkably resistant to change for several generations after arrival.

Gradually, each immigrant altered what historian Maxine Sellers (*To Seek America,* 1977) described as the "values and priorities, ways of expressing (or not expressing) emotion, subtle preferences, and unconscious practices that affected the texture of life in the home, on the job, and in the neighborhood." Many new immigrants who lived in neighborhood replicas of old-world towns, served by familiar merchants and worshipping in the customary style of their groups, felt an intense attachment to their old ways. Others were just as intensely refashioning themselves in the mode of the American Anglo-Saxon Protestant middle class. However, the majority of new immigrants found themselves being pulled in both directions while they tried to design a compromise between total absorption and total alienation.

II

In the period between 1880 and 1921, when the majority of new immigrants arrived, the Federal government neither aided nor interfered with the lives of newcomers after the initial inspection at immigrant reception centers. Immigrants in need of advice or assistance were dependent upon private charities, usually supported by ethnic or religious institutions or by the generosity of individual philanthropists. At first, most of the assistance offered new immigrants came from welfare organizations established by Protestant reformers inspired by the Social Gospel movement or by assimilated members of an ethnic group who now hoped to aid others in making the transition from alien to American.

Operating on the theory that immigrants would be more likely to embrace traditional American values if they were well-fed and well-housed, social reformers set out to remedy the problems of urban life. Protestant Social Gospel reformers established libraries, gymnasiums, soup kitchens, clinics, employment offices, and instructional facilities in a wide variety of subjects. Christians hoping to spread the Gospel through good works reached out to newcomers through the YMCA and YWCA, the Salvation Army, local agencies that provided a broad range of services from emergency food and shelter to health services, and rescue missions for prostitutes, unwed mothers, alcoholics, and other troubled souls.

Church-related programs, by their very nature, often repelled new immigrants. Many social welfare programs designed for the immigrants were thinly disguised missionary efforts. Rather than successfully proselytizing the newcomers, such programs succeeded only in alienating many of them, especially those of Roman Catholic or Jewish faiths. While many of the new imigrants hoped to reconcile their ethnic cultural heritage with this new America lifestyle, most Protestant reformers were bent upon persuading the immigrants to abandon their past and relinquish their old world habits, customs, and native languages. Reformers feared that the divisiveness of a culturally pluralistic society would destroy American democracy, and they considered the religions and values of their clients primitive as compared to progressive Protestant Christianity.

Secular middle-class reformers were frequently more successful in attracting the new immigrants. The fortress from which they launched their assault on poverty and ignorance was the settlement house. These buildings, located in the midst of immigrant enclaves, were run by idealistic social workers who dispensed a wide variety of services to the surrounding neighborhood in the late nineteenth and early twentieth centuries. Jane Addams' Hull House in Chicago (1889), the New York City University Settlement of James B. Reynolds (1886), and the Henry Street Settlement of Lillian Wald (1893) were renowned for their comunity service.

Founded in nineteenth-century England by young, idealistic Cambridge and Oxford men, the settlement movement in the United States was dominated by young college-trained women. These women, often from wealthy backgrounds and of genteel breeding, initially hoped to uplift American society through cultural enrichment of the urban poor. However, music and painting made way for more practical arts in the face of the tremendous needs of new immigrants. Settlements captured the imagination and harnessed the energies of those trained in teaching, social work, nursing, architecture, and urban planning.

The Henry Street Settlement began in 1893 when philanthropists asked a recently graduated nurse, Lillian Wald, to help minister to the needs of poor immigrants on New York's Lower East Side. Wald's experience with poor families visiting patients in the hospital ward where she worked inspired her to draft a course of instruction in home nursing. Her course, first offered in an old building on Henry Street, which had been used as a technical school, inaugurated an expanding program of service. Other settlements had similar beginnings.

Settlement houses provided a comprehensive array of services including counseling, employment bureaus, and emergency relief to those in need of food, clothing, or shelter. There were social clubs for young and old and full schedules of classes in every subject from "Shakespeare" to "English for Beginners," with a wide selection of vocational programs in the industrial arts.

New immigrant children were of particular concern to settlement workers, and reformers were far ahead of their time in developing quality day-care centers to aid working mothers. At settlement houses, children received medical and dental care, nutritious meals, and education. At times, settlement workers carried their efforts into the local public schools as well, teaching immigrant children English and dramatics. Many social workers believed that involving children in theater remedied shyness and helped the children to express their anxieties about life in America. An early friend of the Henry Street Settlement was Yiddish playwright Jacob Gordin, who helped aspiring young actors. "The stage during this period," according to Lillian Wald, "performed its time-honored function of teaching and moralizing."

Classes in cooking helped to acquaint immigrants with American foods and patterns of eating as well as being a culinary exchange. In Milwaukee, settlement workers helped their pupils compile family recipes from Germany, Russia, Poland and elsewhere into *The Settlement Cook Book*. This cookbook, which has been repeatedly revised and reprinted, raised thousands of dollars for the Milwaukee settlement house and is still on the shelf in many American kitchens. But, too frequently, settlement workers ignored the cultural heritages in which immigrants took great pride. Ethnic customs and practices were considered remnants of an old world culture which had no place in America. There was frequently a patronizing, condescending quality to the advice and assistance offered.

Insensitivity to the ethnic rituals and traditions of each respective new immigrant group often did severe damage to reformers' credibility in their communities. In 1910, Jane Addams described one such incident that occurred at Hull House when an abandoned infant died.

A delicate little child was deserted in the Hull House nursery. An investigation showed that it had been born 10 days previously in the Cook County Hospital, but no trace could be found of the unfortunate mother. The little thing lived for several weeks and then, in spite of every care, died. We decided to have it buried by the county and the wagon was to arrive by 11 o'clock. About 9 o'clock in the morning, the rumor of this awful deed reached the neighbors. A half-dozen of them came in a very excited state of mind to protest. They took up a collection out of their poverty with which to defray a funeral. We did not realize that we were really shocking a genuine moral sentiment in the community. In our crudeness, we described the care and tenderness which had been expended upon the little creature while it was alive; that it had every attention from a skilled physician and trained nurse; we even intimated that the excited members of the group had not taken part in this and that it now lay with us to decide that the child should be buried, as it had been born, at the county's expense.

Very quickly Addams and the staff realized their error. Addams lamented

It is doubtful whether Hull House has ever done anything which injured it so deeply in the minds of some of its neighbors. No one born and reared in the community could possibly have made a mistake like that. No one who had studied the ethical standards with any care could have bungled so completely.

Frequently immigrants viewed the efforts of private agencies and philanthropists as unwarranted interference in their lives. Historic experiences aroused suspicion of strangers' altruism. Virginia Yans-McLaughlin, who studied the Italians of Buffalo (*Family and Community,* 1977), explained that the contadini were unaccustomed to "getting something for nothing. Peasants, familiar with poverty, and used to considering it a common problem that everyone in the community shared, considered reliance upon charity even more disgraceful than destitution." Any public or institutional intervention in family life was regarded as an intrusion by contadini in America. Charity was a matter for individuals, not institutions.

All the other new immigrant groups shared the Italians' repugnance toward charity. However, groups such as the Greeks and east European Jews did distinguish between charitable institutions run by members of one's ethnic group and those controlled by outsiders. Only aid from the former was acceptable.

East European Jews were frequently given assistance by organizations established by German Jews who had arrived several generations earlier and were now well-off financially and quite well assimilated. German Jews such as the Schiffs, Lewisohns, and Guggenheims designed their philanthropy to foster rapid assimilation. They wished to eliminate the embarrassing, scruffy, primitive appearance of many east European Jews, especially those who refused to shave their beards and clip their sidelocks.

German philanthropists were generous toward the Hebrew Immigrant Aid Society, but they were even more concerned with founding educational institutions. The most famous of these is the Education Alliance, a synthesis of night school, day-care center, gymnasium, public forum, and settlement house. Irving Howe has described the Alliance as, "a tangible embodiment of the German Jews' desire to help to uplift, clean up, and quiet down their 'coreligionist.'" Some of America's prominent entertainers and educators, such as comedian Eddie Cantor and philosopher Morris Raphael Cohen, owed a debt to the Alliance.

Still, east European Jews were not unaware that the charity of German Jews came at a cost. One Russian Jew complained in a letter to the *Yiddishe Gazetten* in 1894:

In the philanthropic institutions of our aristocratic German Jews you see beautiful offices, desks, all decorated, but strict and angry faces. Every poor man is questioned like a criminal, is looked down upon; every unfortunate suffers self-degradation and shivers like a leaf, just as if he were standing before a Russian official. When the same Russian Jew is in an institution of Russian Jews, no matter how poor and small the building, it will seem to him big and comfortable. He feels at home among his own brothers who speak his tongue, understand his thoughts and feel his heart.

For the destitute, the house of worship was a source of immediate assistance. Religion was often the glue that kept their communities and their own lives together. The Polish Catholic parish in the United States became analogous to the small Polish village or town in the homeland. In addition to providing immigrants with spiritual comfort, houses of worship served as social service centers for ethnic groups. Parish priests became administrators of assistance as well as teachers and spiritual leaders. Community churches took on the task of helping newcomers to adjust emotionally and to find jobs and adequate housing.

Mutual assistance societies, frequently extended more than financial assistance to new immigrants. Members gave one another advice on the practical problems of living in America and the moral support to combat feelings of loneliness and alienation. These societies, or lodges, functioned as burial societies and sponsored insurance plans for members and college scholarships for their children. A fund collected from members' dues aided the unemployed, the ill, and the widows and orphans of deceased members. The burial responsibilities of mutual assistance societies were especially important to immigrants. Newcomers often feared that if they died in America, far from family and friends, they would be put to rest without the rites of their religion, possibly in an unmarked grave. Such societies, and others that were exclusively burial societies, frequently drew members who had been neighbors in the Old World. Now in America, they organized to protect each other from the disgrace of an anonymous grave. Burial society dues were collected— fifty cents, a dollar, at regular intervals—and used to buy a large cemetery plot for members and their families. A modest funeral would also be arranged by the society with appropriate clergy and some society members in attendance. Roman Catholics and orthodox Jews were especially concerned with ritually correct burial because both religions required burial in consecrated ground. The east European Jewish *landsmanschaftn,* or organizations of old country neighbors in America, usually included burial among the services it performed for dues-paying members.

Lodge halls were located in the community where most of the members lived. Meetings were held Sunday afternoon or evening for the benefit of the majority of members who worked six-day weeks and dues were modest, sometimes supplemented by a large donation from a member who had become financially successful. The lodge halls became places for former neighbors to celebrate ethnic holidays, share news of their home towns, and feel at ease.

Whether they belonged to a society or not, immigrants found a corner to meet and share news. They gathered informally in taverns, coffeehouses, shops, and in each other's homes to wrestle with the problems of life in America. They sought advice from those whose success in America qualified them to offer it. In Slavic neighborhoods, tavernkeepers were usually the most prosperous. They were often ex-miners or factory workers who acquired sufficient capital to purchase their own business. New businessmen, politicians, and neighbors patronized their establishments, sharing ideas and information. Whether he turned to brother or uncle, local businessman or social reformer, the immigrant ferreted out the information he needed to make a success of this life in America. Having left his familiar culture behind, he created one in the United States, pulling together pieces of the old and pieces of the new, developing community institutions as the need arose and modifying existing ones to suit his requirements. There were many compromises, but few newcomers surrendered quietly to the dictates of those guidebooks that urged the imigrant to "relinquish his past."

III

By the late nineteenth century, most states had compulsory school attendance laws, though enforcement was erratic. Young newcomers were thus legally required to be in the classroom by day, and frequently their elders voluntarily attended school during the evening. By studying reading, writing, and arithmetic, the children were being tooled to compete for the material rewards America offered. Adults were tutored in English and civics so that they might qualify for citizenship. Some enrolled in vocational programs hoping to acquire skills more immediately applicable to their daily struggle for survival.

Both young and old were subjected to heavy doses of socialization in the classroom, including the importance of cleanliness, hard work, perseverance, individualism, and patriotism. From early morning until late every evening, the public school educators labored to promote assimilation.

Those immigrants who chose to attend formal classes often found the classroom uncomfortable. In 1912, social worker Peter Roberts noted that the young women who taught children during the day often taught adults in the evening but were "not as sympathetic with them as they should be." Too often, Roberts found, "the foreigner contracts the habit of thinking in his mother tongue and then translates his sentences into English," an inefficient method. The teachers did not perceive that immigrants thought in their own language and often attributed to ignorance newcomers' slowness to learn English. The immigrants, repelled by the condescending tone with which such teachers addressed their foreign students, often resisted instruction, clinging to their mother tongues for security. Roberts called for greater sensitivity to the immigrants' needs on the part of educators. As he watched immigrant children enter American classrooms, Roberts was convinced that, "When the public school does (its) work in an efficient manner, it will be one of the most efficient agencies for the assimilation of the men of the new immigration who live in industrial centers."

Many of the immigrants themselves recognized the link between education and Americanization. In her 1912 autobiography, immigrant Mary Antin movingly describes being taken to school, along with her brother and sister, by their father. He knew "no surer way to their advancement and happiness" than education. Antin believed that, for her father, taking his children to school was both a pragmatic and a symbolic gesture. He brought his children to school "as if it were an act of consecration," his way of "taking possession of America."

Not all new immigrants embraced public education with the confidence of Mary Antin's father. Some regarded the schools as American institutions designed to undermine traditional patterns of family life. But, try as they would to resist the incursions of the school on the family, the cultural tug of war was usually won by the school.

In 1910, a woman wrote to editor Abraham Cahan in *The Forward* to complain that her husband disapproved of her going to school two evenings a week, and in retaliation, had imposed strict financial restraints on her. Cahan scolded the husband severely for his behavior and insisted that, "the wife absolutely has the right to go to school two evenings a week." Cahan recognized the role of education in the assimilation process and encouraged his readers to use the schools to their own best advantage, as corridors to the opportunities of American life.

Even those school programs which seemed unexceptional triggered unexpected opposition from immigrants. For instance, state-supported hot lunch programs violated the traditional Italian noontime meal, or *colazione*. It was customary for contadini families to eat together at noon, in the fields or in the home. Lunch programs, designed in particular to help impoverished immigrants, violated the Italian tradition by keeping children away from the family. Often Italian parents insisted that their children come home at noon. Even Richard Gambino, growing up in the 1930s, fondly remembers coming home to a "good home-cooked lunch of the *paise* (old country), for example, fried eggs and potatoes on Italian bread." To Gambino, and to many other youngsters raised in immigrant households, this fare was "indescribably delicious" and much preferred to the school's institutional "balanced meals." However, gradually peer pressure and the insistence of school officials undermined the way of the paise, and Italian children learned to eat away from home.

Rezoning of a school district could place severe constraints on an immigrant group. In 1904, New York City's Board of Education proposed shifting 1,500 children from overcrowded schools in the Lower East Side to less crowded schools on the West Side, according to education historian Diane Ravitch. In angry protest, 2,000 Jewish parents gathered at a settlement house meeting. Of primary concern was the fear that their children would miss morning prayers and afternoon religious school. Jewish parents felt that untempered secular education would inevitably alienate children from their elders.

Often objections raised by an immigrant parent were not confined to the school proper. To a man who objected to his son playing baseball with public school friends in 1903, Abraham Cahan wrote, "It is a mistake to keep children locked up in the house. . . . Bring them up to be educated, ethical and decent, but also to be physically strong, so they should not feel inferior." Baseball was an important part of education because it seemed so American. The game gave Jewish boys a vigorous tie to their fellow countrymen without demanding a sacrifice of Jewish belief and tradition.

Italians, Greeks, and east European Jews sometimes forestalled the Americanization of their children by extending their school days. Italians and Greeks sent their children to parochial schools not only to strengthen their links with their respective churches, but to prevent their children from forgetting completely their distinct heritages. The Greek community organized programs of instruction that followed regular public school classes. These classes, held in church basements and community centers, were designed to teach the Greek language to American-born children. Parents who sent their children to such schools were struggling to temper assimilation so that their children would not become completely alienated from their past. However, according to historian Theodore Saloutos (*The Greeks in the United States,* 1963), the child, "attending public school during the day, in which he was taught by an American-born, American-educated teacher, and then attending a Greek school in the late afternoon, presided over by a Greek-born, Greek-educated teacher, was often confused by the seemingly contradictory experiences." Moreover, most newcomers could not afford the expense of such private schools.

Among east European Jews, Hebrew schools were opened free of charge by philanthropic institutions such as New York's University Settlement and the Educational Alliance. Classes at these Hebrew schools, usually held after public school classes were over for the day, added ethical and religious debate to children's educations through the study of Bible and Jewish traditions. Hebrew schools were a compromise between completely dispensing with Jewish education altogether, and yeshivah training, where the emphasis was upon orthodox Jewish custom and law, and the teachers were rabbis often more fluent in Yiddish than English. Thus, even in the institutions designed to preserve the immigrants' past, the need to adapt to America modified the content and style of education.

Did the public schools actually serve as effective academies of assimilation for the new immigrants? Traditionally, schools have been regarded by historians as the bridge between the Old World and American society. Idealistic teachers guided immigrant children and their parents through the early, difficult stages of assimilation, outfitting students with the intellectual paraphernalia necessary for upward mobility. However, a half century after the end of the new immigration, some historians have embarked upon a revision of this benevolent perspective of the school promoting the immigrant's welfare.

Historian Colin Greer debunks this Great School Legend, suggesting that success in the classroom was not the lever that pried open the door to wealth and prestige in the United States. Greer contends that economic prosperity preceded academic success with "cultural background and economic status being reflected and reinforced in the school, not caused by it." Greer suggests, moreover, that the fundamental purpose of the school was to maintain the relative social positions of groups in the society. Rather than being an agent of Americanization, schools preserved the status quo. School performance, Greer found, consistently depended upon the socioeconomic position of the pupil's family. Immigrant children frequently flunked out of school because the curriculum was designed to weed out those unable to conform to the white Protestant model of success and achievement.

On balance, the public school system was neither the only path to economic and social opportunities nor a reactionary institution designed to perpetuate the existing class structure. Importantly, education had a different significance and usefulness for each new immigrant group. And the nature of the relationship between the child and the school was perhaps more a function of the immigrant's unique cultural attitudes than the design of the institution. As with mobility studies, historians have been as yet unable to adequately measure the attitudes of new immigrant groups toward education. Figures on school attendance or academic failures for each group are insufficient measures of immigrant attitudes toward the schools. Such data may reveal more about a group's success in surmounting obstacles to education than they do about whether group members regarded the educational process as benign or detrimental to their best interests in America.

The importance of cultural perspective was pointed up in a study of the scholastic achievement of immigrant children in urban schools between 1900 and 1930 by Michael R. Olneck and Marvin Lazerson ("The School Achievement of Immigrant Children: 1900–1930," *History of Education Quarterly,* Winter 1974). In the east European Jewish community, study and learning were highly valued. The practice of Judaism required literacy, and a mark of family success was the ability to educate the male children in Talmudic law and the rabbinic commentaries on the law. Religious schools were scattered throughout the Pale and, in larger cities, there were often great *yeshivat,* centers of Jewish learning. This traditional respect for learning and confidence in educational institutions survived the journey to America and expanded to include secular public schools.

In contrast, the researchers found that southern Italian culture placed low priority on formal education. In the Mezzogiorno, family loyalty was the greatest virtue and the most important duty. The outside influence of school which encouraged individualistic success and upward mobility appeared to be a direct challenge to family values and parental control. Contadini in the streets of America reminded each other of the southern Italian proverb: "Stupid and contemptible is he who makes his children better than himself." Moreover, long hours in the classroom prevented the young from contributing to the family coffers, as had been the custom in Italy. As one resentful parent said, "The schools (make) of our children persons of leisure—little gentlemen. They (lose) the dignity of good children to think just of the parents, to help them. . . ."

Thomas Kessner's study of mobility among New York's Italian and east European Jewish immigrants (1977) examines New York City public school surveys from 1908 and 1910 to suggest the influence of cultural attitudes upon performance. In 1908, a survey of fifteen Manhattan schools showed a disproportionately high number of immigrant children left behind one or more grades. Among the new immigrants, 23 percent of the east European Jewish children were left behind as compared with 36 percent of the Italian children. The study focusing on those who successfully completed high school found that none of the Italians who entered high school graduated, while 16 percent of the east European children received diplomas. A 1910 survey of New York's slums cited by Kessner found more Jews above age sixteen still in school than any other ethnic group. Six years later, a census of local colleges revealed that the Jewish enrollment constituted 73 percent of the City College student body.

More than any other immigrant group Jewish immigrants took advantage of New York's free city colleges. Newspapers reported that "the thirst for knowledge . . . fills our city colleges and Columbia's halls with the sons of Hebrews who came over in steerage . . . ." Aware of the trend, Italian journalists and educators urged their *compari,* "Let us do as the Jews . . . invade the schools, teach ourselves, have our children taught, open to them the school paths by means of the hatchet of knowledge and genius . . . ."

John W. Briggs in *An Italian Passage, Immigrants to Three American Cities, 1840–1930,* suggests that Italian parents viewed education warily only so long as they believed that their families' residence in America would be temporary. Once committed to America as their permanent home, Italians valued education just as highly as any other group. Briggs spotlighted elementary-school children in Rochester, Utica, and Kansas City. He found that Italian children had roughly the same attendance patterns as other immigrant and native-born students. In Rochester, where data were available, Briggs discovered that Italian children did not experience unusually high rates of failures.

Controversy continues to perk over southern Italian attitudes toward education in the United States. Some, such as Kessner, argue that southern Italians disdained education, while others such as Briggs contend that no cultural differences existed between Italians and other groups over the value of schooling. Instead, Briggs reports that many Italian immigrants had middle-class values and aspirations, including an enthusiasm for education. Only their own desire to return to Italy rather than remain in the United States, he reports, kept southern Italians from encouraging their children to pursue scholastic success. Once reconciled to remaining in America, however, Italians were as eager for their children to become highly educated as any other group.

Again, as with studies of upward mobility, much of the debate over education may result from historians asking the wrong questions. An assumption has been made by scholars that a link existed between education and an individual's ability to make good in America. It has also been assumed that immigrants saw this connection clearly; thus the debate on education eventually dovetails back into the debate over mobility, with much counting of students and comparisons between ethnic groups. Instead, historians should consider education within the context of the overall cultural perspective of each immigrant group. The issue is less school attendance of Italians as compared to Jews, but school attendance of Italians in Italy, immediately after coming to America, and later in ensuing generations.

The public school was the subject of much ambivalence in the new immigrant communities. While some regarded the classroom as the gateway to success, others perceived it as an insidious back door to assimilation which lured the young from the ways of their parents. In fact it was often both simultaneously.

But above all, the school was the great storehouse of American culture and habits. Each immigrant group entered with its own shopping list, picking and choosing, and paying in the coinage of compromise and assimilation.

I V

Told to speak a new language, learn a new skill, let the children be baseball players, keep house like an American, eat differently, dress differently—it seemed as though nothing short of total transformation would make the immigrant acceptable to this alien society. However, those who settled in large cities found the American political process neither censorious nor distant and aloof. The masters of party politics liked the immigrant just fine. In the districts and wards that made up the immigrant neighborhood, urban bosses and their associates attended lodge meetings, festas, and funerals. They mingled in bars and coffeehouses frequented by particular immigrant groups. Always the boss provided food to the hungry and shelter to the homeless. Newcomers low on cash were more than willing to repay the boss—at the ballot box.

The immigrant's importance to the urban politician was established long before the onset of the new immigration in 1880. During the 1840s and 1850s, politicians in both major parties looked greedily at the millions of Irish and German immigrants, knowing that most of the males would soon be casting ballots. The Irish vote soon became the cornerstone of Democratic support in New York and many other large eastern cities. In the small communities of the Midwest, both major parties contended for the German vote. The immigrant ballot became for politicians the key to partisan hegemony.

The first bosses that the new immigrants encountered were often Irish. These successful heirs of white Protestant politicians seemed to have an instinctive understanding of their varied constituencies. Bosses such as Honest John Kelly and Richard Croker of New York, James McManus of Philadelphia, and

Christopher Magee and William Finn of Pittsburgh, all immigrants themselves or the sons of immigrants, recognized the economic and psychological needs of the newcomers. Democratic headquarters in New York, Tammany Hall, run by Mayor Fernando Wood in the 1850s, had offered to Irish immigrants baskets of coal in winter, turkeys at Thanksgiving, and most importantly, patronage jobs on the police force and on publicly financed construction projects. Now forty years later, ward bosses provided the same services to Italians, Slavs, and east European Jews: emergency food and fuel, legal assistance, and, of course, jobs that new arrivals could get nowhere else as quickly or with as few explanations.

Urban bosses were especially sensitive to the diverse ethnic customs and traditions in their wards. George Washington Plunkitt, a Tammany boss in New York City at the turn of the century, gave a series of humorous, colorful, and highly informative interviews on machine politics that were published in newspapers and later as a book. Plunkitt acknowledged the need to accept ethnic differences among his constituents and act accordingly. One of his functionaries was Johnnie Ahearn of the fourth district who had a constituency that was half Irish and half Jewish. Plunkitt admired Ahearn's ability to remain popular with both groups, "He eats corned beef and kosher meat with equal nonchalance, and it's all the same to him whether he takes off his hat in the church or pulls it down over his ears in the synagogue." Both Ahearn and Plunkitt understood that assimilation was a slow, halting, and painful process. They knew that immigrants were most supportive of politicians who were sensitive to their desire to retain their ethnic identities as they adjusted to life in America.

There was a price tag on the assistance and support provided by urban bosses and their efficient organizations. The naturalized immigrant was expected to vote for the candidates nominated by the bosses' party. The power of bosses within their parties was based upon their ability to generate support within this new voting population. As they were called to the polls by party workers, the voters were reminded of Johnnie

Ahearn's good manners or of the patronage job gratefully received.

Unpleasant memories of those who made and enforced the law in their native countries made many new immigrants hesitant at first to have any contact with politics or politicians. However, the humane assistance and warm, personal style of many bosses and their associates soon dispelled such wariness. Bosses tempered economic assistance with friendship and respect and those who accepted their aid did not, therefore, feel diminished by it. The machine thus eased the strain of assimilation. Soon members of new immigrant groups themselves tried the political waters, often using the machine to launch their own careers.

Many opposition politicians, journalists, and public spirited reformers deplored what they regarded as the opportunism of urban bosses. In *Shame of the Cities* (1904), reformer Lincoln Steffens condemned bossism as undemocratic. However, social workers who aided the urban poor perceived the important function of the boss and his machine at the community level. Jane Addams, in the early twentieth century, understood why bosses succeeded where reformers failed:

Primitive people such as the southern Italian peasants who live in the 9th ward, deep down in their hearts admire nothing so much as a good man. The successful candidate must be a good man according to the standards of his constituents. He must not attempt to hold up a morality beyond them, nor must he attempt to reform or change the standard.

Still many reformers, concerned more about preserving morality in government than assisting new arrivals, pursued efforts to curb the power of the machine. As machine politicians sought to educate newcomers in their style of politics, Andrew Dickson White, president of Cornell University said, "With very few exceptions, the city governments of the United States are the worst in Christendom—the most expensive, the most inefficient, and the most corrupt." White and others demanded reform. In 1883, the National Civil Service Reform League and other revisionist groups succeeded in gaining passage of the Pendleton Act, which organized civil service appointments on a merit system in an effort to curb federal patronage positions, the meat that sustained the machine. However, bosses and their allies were strong enough to manipulate the civil service lists to keep their friends in office and prevent their enemies from enjoying the spoils of office after a victory.

As a Progressive reformer in the 1890s Theodore Roosevelt studied the machine and concluded that urban reformers would have to create whole social agencies to fulfill the role of the boss before he could be displaced. However, not until the New Deal was created by distant cousin Franklin, did his idea of social agencies become a reality. Meanwhile, the machine thrived.

Opportunists or not, political bosses usually provided urban groups with badly needed services and used their power to stimulate urban growth even as they enriched themselves and enhanced their party's political fortunes. These partisan warriors and their morally ambiguous machinations have defied all efforts to render a clear-cut judgment of their record. Many an urban boss derived money and patronage while meeting the needs of the city for expanded public utilities—water, gas, transportation, and electricity—as well as the construction of public buildings, sewage systems, docks, and street and sidewalk pavements. Many also markedly increased the number of schools, hospitals, museums, and other institutions and services needed by an expanding city. In the process, bosses had to circumvent city charters that saddled city government with archaic legislative machinery, weak executive authority, and disorganized courts. Whether they were scoundrels masquerading as angels of mercy or urban Robin Hoods, bosses surmounted obstacles to their constituents' welfare. And often those whom they served best were the newest, neediest, and most numerous of their constituents—the immigrants.

The new immigrants did not usually embrace partisan politics immediately or eagerly. Their old-world experiences left members of many groups suspicious of government and distrustful of those who pursued political power. However, the urban boss and his lieutenants fanned out across cities, burrowing into the districts and wards where immigrants lived. From them, the immigrants gradually learned to bend the political system to their own ends wherever they could muster a majority at the ballot box.

But political savvy was only one American trait. Between 1880 and 1921 many newcomers had already learned a new language, altered their dress, adjusted to new marriage roles, changed their dietary habits, and modified their styles of religious worship. They were remaking themselves into Americans—or as close to Americans as they chose to be. And most found the change profound and unsettling, one that might take most of a lifetime to become accustomed to.

Yet, to native-born Americans, the metamorphosis was almost imperceptible. Many found the appearance and behavior of the newcomers repulsive—and very frightening. Just the vast size of the immigration was altering the nation in a rapid, uncontrolled fashion. At best, immigrants appeared to be naive greenhorns; at worst, foreign interlopers. To many Americans, the new immigrants would always be aliens. And to many immigrants the native-born would always seem reluctant hosts.

These divergent perceptions of the immigrants' entry into American society were reflected in the mixed reviews that greeted Israel Zangwill's play, *The Melting Pot,* when it opened before its first American audience at Washington, D.C.'s Columbia Theater in 1908. Zangwill, a British Jew, told the story of young David Quixano, a Jewish immigrant who fled to the United States from Russia following his family's slaughter in a pogrom. As the plot unfolds, David writes a great symphony and falls in love with another immigrant, a Gentile Russian noblewoman. In the final scene, the symphony receives great acclaim and the young immigrant wins the lady. Despite the injunctions of Jewish law against intermarriage, the hero decides to follow the dictates of his heart and marry her.

Advocates of an American melting pot praised the play, especially President Theodore Roosevelt, seated next to the playwright's wife on opening night. To Roosevelt, immigrant languages and cultures were obstacles to American nationalism and impediments to the welfare of newcomers in their new country. He contended that

The man who becomes completely Americanized—who celebrates our constitutional Centennial instead of the Queen's Jubilee, or the Forth of July rather than St. Patrick's Day and who talks 'United States' instead of the dialect of the country which he has of his own free will abandoned—is not only doing his plain duty by his adopted land, but is also rendering himself a service of immeasurable value.

The melting-pot concept flattered American vanity. It suggested not only that the nation was a haven for the oppressed, but that when refugees were exposed to American democracy they underwent a dramatic metamorphosis for the better. There emerged a distinctly new type—the American—who was culturally and biologically superior to the people of Europe and Asia from whom the American was distilled.

However, the praise for Zangwill's *Melting Pot* was less than unanimous. Immigrant newspapers panned the play as an overly idealized version of the assimilation process. The Jewish immigrant press, in particular, took exception to the endorsement of intermarriage as an acceptable vehicle of assimilation. These critics were irritated by the image of newly arrived immigrants standing down at the docks with those of their own kind—each group with its language and history, its particular hatreds and rivalries—soon to be mixed together indiscriminately for the good of all. As early as the first act, Zangwill has David observe that "America is God's Crucible, the great Melting Pot where all the races of Europe are melting and reforming!" By the last act the melting pot is touted as Americanism as David exclaims, "A fig for your feuds and vendettas! Germans and Frenchmen, Irishmen and Englishmen, Jews and Russians—into the crucible with you all! God is making the American." To those who had experienced religious prejudice and discrimination or who had witnessed conflict among immigrants of diverse background, the melting-pot image hardly seemed to reflect their experience in the United States. And it offended millions of immigrants who hoped to amicably reconcile their native culture with their new surroundings, not to drown their past and resurface as Americans.

Equally outraged by Zangwill's play were those native-born who did not share President Roosevelt's confidence in the melting process. Even as the immigrants rejected the concept of a melting pot as undesirable and threatening, Americans intimidated by the size and character of the new immigration denounced the policy of assimilatio.ı. They wanted protection from this foreign intrusion that they perceived was a menace to their values, institutions, economic stability, and self-image.

FIVE

Nativism and the End of Unlimited Entry

A popular immigrant slogan ran, "America beckons, but Americans repel." The new immigrants confronted substantial and escalating hostility in the period 1880 to 1921, even as urban politicians plotted to capture the immigrant vote and industrialists relished the abundance of cheap, unskilled immigrant labor for their factories. Ever since the mass migration of Irish and Germans to the United States in the mid-nineteenth century, immigrants had encountered the suspicion and trepidation of those already in America. The opposition that the new immigrants faced was thus an extension of an already established pattern.

Those antagonistic to the immigrants were not merely a small coterie of mindless bigots. Millions of Americans were intimidated by the size and diversity of the foreign intrusion and by 1921 welcomed federal legislation that finally dammed the flow from abroad. They had specific grounds for objecting to these newcomers. The majority of immigrants were either Catholic or Jewish, especially frightening to a predominantly Protestant America. Moreover, almost all newcomers were emigrating from nondemocratic societies, where republicanism and personal liberty were not time-honored traditions. Many immigrants were leery of law and government as institutions which had always catered to their rulers. To Americans, for whom the law was a sacred trust and a legacy from the patriots of the Revolution, the unfamiliarity of the immigrants with the ways of democracy and their general mistrust of government loomed as a tangible threat to the continuation of American republican government.

The physical appearance of the newcomers, over which they had little control, was perhaps most frightening to the native-born. Among the immigrants were men, women, and children weakened by malnutrition, their bodies deformed by vitamin deficiencies. Those who continued to wear their native garb for a time appeared out of place and even a bit ominous in the streets of America's new modern cities. Just as the ragged Irish of an earlier era had made proper Bostonians cringe, so the new immigrants of every hue and body type met anxious glances as they tramped down gangplanks into a New World long dominated by Anglo-Saxons. With each succeeding boatload, Americans worried about the influence of foreign blood on the vitality of the American population.

Even as the new immigrant found employment and made his peace with his strange, new environment, he faced the distrust and animosity of both the native-born and the immigrants of an earlier era. While he sought to broaden his options and opportunities in the United States, they moved to narrow his choices and choke off possibilities of advancement. In 1921, it seemed that the immigrants had lost the last round; the imposition of federal immigration quotas by frightened Americans abruptly curtailed the growth of the immigrant community. However, the immigrants won the bout. Neither the Congress nor those who had lobbied against immigration could oust those already here, nor could they arrest the changes new immigrants had already initiated in their adopted homeland.

I

As they began arriving in the early 1880s, the new immigrants confronted hostility from a traditional source of anti-immigrant sentiment, the nativists. Most broadly defined, nativists were those Americans who believed that the immigrants posed an imminent danger to their way of life and who spoke out or acted against this "alien menace." From early on, the new immigrants were the targets of nativist intellectuals concerned with such issues as how best to preserve political democracy, defend individual liberties, maintain respect for the law, and preserve the purity of the Anglo-Saxon race. Immigrants were denounced in articles and books most newcomers could not yet read and derided in sermons from church pulpits and university lecterns most never heard.

Most serious in its effect was the hostility generated by rank-and-file nativists who deplored the threat they believed newcomers posed to their economic and social position. These were not wild-eyed reactionaries, but a broad spectrum of sober, middle-class Americans who dreaded job competition from alien workers, bemoaned the congestion of cities crammed with foreigners, and distrusted strangers who spoke other languages and lived lives that seemed so peculiar.

Of course strangers are regarded with suspicion in all societies. However, for most of America's history, its population was remarkably homogeneous; white, Anglo-Saxon, and Protestant. Religious and racial minorities had little if any direct influence in shaping America's economic and political traditions. Most Americans attributed their cherished liberties to twin roots: the Anglo-Saxon tradition embodied in the Magna Carta, that primal expression of political democracy, and the Protestant Reformation, the spiritual rebellion against an oppressive Roman Catholic Church. From America's shores, what were considered the tyrannical monarchies of Europe and the oppressive influence of the Roman Catholic Church seemed too distant to be threatening. Then, in the middle of the nineteenth century, Irish Catholics arrived in large numbers and native Americans began to be uneasy. This unease grew to absolute anxiety with the new immigration at the end of the century.

Natives and newcomers viewed each other through a prism of racial, religious, and cultural rivalries. Still, most Americans and most early immigrants were willing to coexist, however warily. But, the new immigrants, even more alien than the Irish, stirred latent fears that a time was coming when a majority of the population would no longer be of Anglo-Saxon Protestant stock. Nativism was the response of those Americans who, latching onto this fear, regarded themselves as an endangered species and were prepared to be ruthless in their own self-defense.

The immigrants, then, were under attack for reasons that can be isolated for analytical purposes, though many Americans had multiple reasons for despising the newcomers. John Higham, in his now classic study of nativism, *Strangers in the Land* (1955), identified three strains of anti-immigrant venom: racial nativism, anti-Catholicism, and antiradical nativism. However, anti-Semitism, its origins buried deep in the culture of Western civilization, might well be treated as a fourth strain. Then, too, immigrants encountered the hatred of those who blamed the newcomers for unemployment, low wages, or urban problems such as violent crime and vice.

The racial nativism which new immigrants inspired in their hesitant hosts was most frequently expressed in the books written by self-appointed guardians of America's Anglo-Saxon heritage, who were frequently scientists or college professors. Many of these scholars were inspired by Charles Darwin's biological research, arguing that Darwin's hypothesis on the physical evolution of plants and animals was applicable to the evolution of human society as well. They mistakenly applied Darwin's biological theories on the "survival of the fittest" to society. Though Darwin meant only that some species would be more adaptable to a particular environment than others, nativists interpreted "fittest" and "best." Confident that certain races would triumph over inferior competitors because of a natural fitness, an inherent superiority, they insisted that heredity alone determined which species could and which could not adapt to democratic forms of government and the competition of the free enterprise system. To establish which members of the species were most fit, some researchers compared the cranial volumes of human skulls from members of various ethnic groups. Others used "Intelligence Quotient" tests. These measurements and observations were undeliberately culture-bound, favoring people most like the individual who had designed the questions and tasks. Nevertheless, investigators contended that science ratified their prejudices.

At the turn of the century, economist Francis Walker, President of the Massachusetts Institute of Technology, described the newcomers as "beaten men from beaten races," and quite unlike "those who are descended from the tribes that met under the oak trees of Old Germany to make laws and choose chieftains."

Edward Alsworth Ross, a professor of sociology at the University of Wisconsin, in *The Old World in the New* (1914) concluded that the immigrants were subcommon and that they would racially cripple the American population if permitted unrestricted entry. His investigation consisted primarily of observation and he drew an absolute connection between "different" and "inferior."

Observe immigrants not as they come travel-worn up to the gang-plank, nor as they issue toil-begrimed from pit's mouth or mill gate, but in their gatherings, washed, combed, and in their Sunday best. You are struck by the fact that from ten to twenty percent are hirsute, low-browed, big-faced persons of obviously low mentality. . . . These oxlike men are descendants of those who always stayed behind.

Ross's observations and conclusions were echoed by many others with similar credentials and equally primitive research methods.

Madison Grant's *The Passing of the Great Race* (1916) synthesized many racial nativist arguments into a masterful and widely read treatise on the superiority of hereditary over environmental factors in shaping mankind. Grant amassed much scientific data but interpreted it through the prism of his own prejudices. He insisted that race mixing produced a hybrid race that reverted to a "more ancient, generalized and lower type." The lowest type among the immigrants was the east European Jew. The antithesis of the tall, fair Nordic type most admired by Grant, east European Jews could only sap the Anglo-Saxon race of its vitality if permitted to enter the United States and intermarry.

Lothrop Stoddard, a New England attorney trained in history, echoed Grant, claiming that yellow- and brown-skinned peoples were inherently inferior to Caucasians. In *The Rising Tide of Color* (1920) he warned that racially inferior nonwhites actively sought to undermine the civilization created by whites of Teutonic and Anglo-Saxon heritage. Other nativists claimed to have confirmed Grant's hypothesis with their own primitive I.Q. tests. However, they ignored evidence that contradicted their assumptions, such as test results which demonstrated that the longer a group lived in the United States, the higher its members scored on I.Q. tests.

The monitions of Grant and other nativists that new immigrants represented a clear and present danger to the physical vitality of Americans and to the survival of American institutions did not go unchallenged. In 1911, Columbia University anthropologist Franz Boas, himself a German Jewish immigrant, published *The Mind of Primitive Man,* an extensive refutation of racial nativism. In one series of experiments, Boas demonstrated that the American environment was modifying the very "racial characteristics" that nativists had found so detestable in the new immigrants. Because the slope of the cranium was often regarded as a reliable index of race, he measured the skulls of second-generation immigrants and discovered that many no longer physically resembled their parents' generation. Long-headed types grew shorter and round-headed types often developed elongated heads. Boas concluded that nutrition and other aspects of living conditions determined these "racial characteristics" more than heredity. Though Boas was acclaimed in the scientific community, he never convinced the lay readers who preferred scientific studies that supported rather than refuted their rationale for nativism.

Catholic immigrants from Italy, Poland, Greece, Mexico, and Canada were confronted by hatred distilled from faith and history, rather than science. Anti-Catholicism was imported by the first English Protestants who had settled along the Atlantic coast in the seventeenth century. Themselves the products of the Protestant Reformation, these Englishmen regarded the Pope as a foreign tyrant wielding dangerous international influence. The authoritarian organization of the Roman Catholic Church, its link to feudal or monarchical governments in Spain and France, and Henry VIII's schism with the Church during the sixteenth century all contributed to America's anti-Catholic heritage.

The publication in 1885 of *Our Country: Its Possible Future and Its Present Crisis* by Protestant minister Josiah Strong stoked anti-Catholic nativism. Strong identified "an irreconcilable difference between papal principles and the fundamental principles of our free institutions." He viewed the urban political machine, often run by Irish Catholic politicians courting the votes of the new immigrants, as just the first of many pernicious influences that the newcomers would exert on American society.

Anti-Catholicism declined in the 1890s, but Jewish immigrants from eastern Europe continued to experience a nativism grounded in ancient religious antipathies. Traditionally, anti-Semitism was based on the orthodox Christian view of Jews as God's Chosen People who betrayed their Lord. In the late nineteenth century, however, anti-Semitic nativism in the United States was more economc than religious in origin. The Shylock image of the usurious Jew, popularized by Shakespeare's "Merchant of Venice," peppered the speeches and writings of American agrarian and labor leaders, as well as the stewards of established wealth who feared the social changes brought about by industrialization, urbanization, and immigration. There was also a racial component to anti-Semitic nativism. Sociologist E. A. Ross suggested in 1914 that Jews might be unable to compete as equals in the American economy because they were "the polar opposite of our pioneer breed." He and others complained that not only were Jews undersized and weak-muscled, but "they shun bodily activity and are exceedingly sensitive to pain." Economics and racial inferiority were linked by anti-Semites who claimed that the physically inferior Jew compensated for his difference with cunning and avariciousness in the marketplace.

Anti-Semitism was voiced by many early twentieth century educators, including Goldwin Smith, Cornell University's distinguished historian. Smith defended Europe's exclusion of Jews from political equality with Gentiles. According to Smith, ". . . it may be fairly asked whether the member of a parasitic race, preserving his tribalism and tribal interests, had a plain and unmistakable right to a share of political power in a community to which he could hardly be said to belong." Smith's opposition to Jewish immigration was echoed by Henry Adams, Henry Cabot Lodge, and many contemporaries.

Immigrants occasionally found themselves under attack for political as well as racial and religious reasons. Though there was no evidence that most immigrants were radicals or came to America to foment revolution, the handful who did participate in labor protests or wrote in support of socialism or anarchism only seemed to confirm preexisting nativist apprehensions. By the late nineteenth century, antiradical nativism had become an American perennial. Thomas Jefferson in *Notes on the State of Virginia* (1781) had observed that most immigrants would necessarily come from despotic countries and would either retain those undemocratic principles of the government or would pass to the other extreme and degenerate into anarchy. Though Jefferson and other Americans applauded the French Revolution in 1789 and avidly followed other revolutionary movements, especially in Latin America, it was feared that political refugees seeking sanctuary in the United States might be either too reactionary or too radical to nourish the gains of the American Revolution.

The Haymarket Riot of 1886, which followed a protest meeting called by labor organizers and anarchist agitators, involved many of Chicago's immigrant workers. It called attention to the radicalism of some immigrants. The incident stoked the fears of those already leery of working side by side with "strangers." Despite apprehensions, most newcomers were too preoccupied with adjusting to their new environment to consider subversive political activity of any kind. Moreover, many immigrants abhorred radical socialism; socialists advocated curbing immigration to prevent cheap immigrant labor from depressing American wages.

The majority of new immigrants entered the American economy as unskilled laborers, competing for jobs with native-born workers and immigrants from northern and western Europe. Factories and mines, thus, became tinderboxes scattered over the American landscape. Labor strikes and work shortages were the sparks which ignited nativist violence. American workers cared little about the esoteric arguments of nativist scientists and college professors. They found their own practical reasons for hating the newcomers.

The most systematic campaign against any new immigrant group was that mounted on the west coast against the Chinese. Nineteenth-century Americans regarded Chinese culture as primitive, Chinese society as backward, and Chinese influence upon democratic institutions as corrosive. Considered racially inferior heathens, the Chinese were stigmatized as the "Yellow Peril" as they began to settle in some numbers on the Pacific Coast. It required only an economic crisis to transform latent prejudices into an all-out anti-Chinese crusade. During the national depression of 1870, easterners traveled west on the newly-completed transcontinental railroad, hoping to buy farm land or claim mining stakes. Instead they found themselves confronted with speculative land prices and in competition with the Chinese immigrants for a handful of unpalatable jobs. In 1871, rioters killed twenty-one Chinese in San Francisco; in 1877, twenty-five Chinese laundries were burned. Such violence was echoed in Colorado and Wyoming and during the following decade reverberated throughout the western states.

Other immigrant groups as well were the targets of violent reactions to economic stress. In 1895, during a labor strike in the southern Colorado coal fields, a gang of miners and townspeople killed six Italian laborers implicated in the death of a native-born saloonkeeper. Heavily indebted Louisiana farmers went on a rampage against Jewish merchants, while in Mississippi local hoodlums burned and destroyed the homes of Jewish landlords.

The Leo Frank case demonstrates how economic tensions could be fused with other genres of nativism. Leo Frank was the Cornell University educated son of Russian Jews. His father was a New York manufacturer and Leo came to the South to manage a pencil factory in Atlanta. Despite thin evidence, Frank was found guilty of murdering a young factory worker, Mary Phagan, in 1914. He was denounced by local residents, journalists, and politicians for exploiting southern workers and besmirching the South's womanhood. When the governor commuted his sentence to life, some Georgians boycotted Jewish-owned stores; others formed an explosive mob, stormed the jail, and lynched Frank.

Immigrants were blamed for social as well as economic disorders that burdened American society, especially those in urban areas where most of the newcomers settled. Statistics on soaring crime rates in neighborhoods with high concentrations of immigrants were held up by nativist journalists, reformers, and politicians as proof positive of the deleterious influence of the immigrant on his environment. However, further investigation has suggested to historians a more complex interpretation of such figures.

Because taverns, gambling houses, and brothels were usually not tolerated in the more refined neighborhoods of the native-born, they often could exist untroubled by the law only in immigrant enclaves. In such establishments, immigrants sought temporary escape from cramped quarters and gray, depressing lives. Each group had a favorite vice. Slavs and Italians favored drinking more than Jews, who preferred gambling as did the Chinese. But no group had a monopoly on any particular vice. Though approximately 50 percent of the prostitutes in large urban areas were immigrants or the daughters of immigrants, they numbered the native-born among their customers.

Settlement workers were perhaps more realistic than journalists or policemen in acknowledging that abominable living conditions, sickness, fear, and loneliness were the real causes of crime. Most of the arrests were for crimes of poverty such as drunkenness, vagrancy, or petty theft. Social workers argued that the thief who stole small amounts of food, clothing, or money was desperately attempting to cope with poverty and hopelessness, rather than responding to an innate criminality. Despite charges by some native Americans, the facts suggest that the criminality of foreign-born in America was no larger than that of native-born. In September, 1909, only 25 percent of the prisoners in New York's Sing Sing Prison were foreign-born, although immigrants comprised over 43 percent of New York City's total population.

Yet the myth of the immigrant criminality persisted. In 1913, Peter Roberts traced the cause to "drink and housing conditions." Roberts, an advocate of temperance, condemned those who "sacrifice their reason to Bacchus." Different new immigrant groups were stereotypically linked by the native-born to certain kinds of crimes. The Italians and Greeks were accused of "a distinct tendency to abduction and kidnapping"; the Russians, to "larceny and receiving stolen goods."

The 1911 report of the United States Immigration Commission charged that "certain kinds of criminality are inherent in the Italian race." The criminal activities of the mafia, or Black Hand, had led undiscriminating investigators to make a sweeping generalization defaming an entire group.

In his 1970 study of the Italian community in Chicago, historian Humbert Nelli contended that organized crime had existed in Chicago long before the arrival of the Italians. The city's organized crime began in the 1870s under the leadership of Irish hoodlums such as Michael Cassius McDonald. The "Black Hand" was not a vast Italian syndicate, according to Nelli, but a style of extortion used by small groups of Italian hoodlums to squeeze money from superstitious, frightened Italian workers. Only later, in the 1920s, did Chicago Italians play a major role in syndicate criminal activities, profiting from Prohibition violations, prostitution, gambling, and drug sales. In another book (*The Business of Crime,* 1976), Nelli demonstrated that the original Sicilian "mafia" floundered in America, only "the secrecy, rituals, and exotic behavior" of the old-world criminal societies remained. But these old-world criminal rites and symbols titillated the American imagination and caused the press to credit the hoodlums with "wondrous evil power," far beyond their real capabilities.

Throughout the period 1880–1921, then, the new immigrants met with criticism and resistance. Traditional prejudice rooted in racial and religious differences survived the journey to the New World, though the ancient hatreds were frequently cloaked in the modern jargon of science. Self-appointed guardians of democracy and the national morality armed themselves with arguments borrowed from the founding fathers and Biblical text. Rational discourse and biblical parable, appropriately tailored to suit the audience, thus fueled hostility between native and newcomer. However, American workers, justifiably fearful of immigrant job competition and contemptuous of alien strikebreakers hardly needed science or religion to feed their animosity toward the new immigrants. Many Americans, dissatisfied with individually denouncing the newcomers or joining in random incidents of resistance, turned to collective efforts to halt immigration and limit the influence of those already here.

II

Newly-arrived immigrants found that even as many charities, churches, political parties, and immigrant aid societies welcomed them, other groups were equally dedicated to slamming

America's "golden door" in their faces. Nativists lobbied in the halls of Congress and state legislatures, sometimes running political candidates on anti-immigrant platforms. Often terrorist intimidation was substituted for political opposition. Organized anti-immigrant campaigns were limited neither geographically nor socioeconomically. In various regions of the United States, nativist groups and leaders stepped forward to oppose immigration, often focusing their efforts on a particular immigrant group settled in their region of the country.

One of the earliest opponents of a new immigrant group was himself an immigrant. Dennis Kearney, an Irish-born sailor who had dabbled unsuccessfully in mining speculation, saw Chinese immigrants as scapegoats for his personal debacle and targeted them for a demagogic crusade in the late 1870s. Kearney's racist campaign began in San Francisco's sandlots, but soon spread as newspapers thundered his anti-Chinese rhetoric. He charged that the Chinese were in deliberate collusion with large corporate enterprises against white workers, accepting slave wages in return for a monopoly on jobs. Kearney always ended his diatribes by proclaiming, "The Chinese must go!" and his audiences responded with alacrity.

Kearney in 1877 organized the Workingmen's party to harness to politics the vigor of his reactionary movement. Too small to actually field its own candidates, the Workingmen's party operated as a voting bloc just large enough to hold the balance of power in California, a state crucial to both Republicans and Democrats in national elections. The demands of Kearney's party were specific: cut off Chinese immigration and curtail the legal and economic rights of those already in the United States.

At first, politicans were leery of associating themselves with the fanatically racist Workingmen's Party. Moreover, they were hampered by the 1868 Burlingame Treaty with China, which guaranteed extensive privileges to Chinese citizens in the United States in return for highly favorable trade concessions to American merchants. Yet, by 1876, a California legislative committee had proclaimed the Chinese racially inferior, people without souls or with souls not worth saving. And, in 1880, the Burlingame Treaty was revised so that the U.S. could regulate, limit, or suspend Chinese immigration, though it could not technically prohibit it. To circumvent the treaty, proponents of exclusion introduced a bill suspending the immigration of Chinese laborers for ten years; this became the Chinese Exclusion Act of 1882. The law was renewed periodically until 1945.

With the passage of each new bill, the anti-Chinese crusade grew stronger and its nativist missionaries more exultant. All Chinese living in the United States were required to obtain a certificate from the Chinese Consul General and a second document from the immigration inspector at San Francisco. Likewise, all Chinese entering the country for the first time were required to carry certification from the Chinese government. Any error in the paperwork generally meant exclusion or deportation.

Though only ten Chinese were admitted into the U.S. in 1887, Republicans pushed through passage of the Scott Act which expressly prohibited Chinese laborers from coming to the U.S. and limited acceptable immigrants to five classes: officials, teachers, students, merchants, and tourists. More importantly, the Act broadly defined "Chinese" as any member of the "Chinese race," whether or not they were Chinese nationals. And, most tragically, the Act prohibited the return of any Chinese who had left the United States. Despite their ownership of American property and their families' residence in this country, 20,000 Chinese laborers who had returned to China for a visit were denied readmission. Many never saw their families again.

Chinese living in the United States endured abuse and indignity. Discrimination in housing and occupations was unrelenting and slanderous images of the Chinese were splashed through the newspapers. The American public was told that the Chinese were opium merchants, prostitutes, gamblers, and members of frightening, illegal secret societies. Those who wore queues (pigtails) were the objects of scorn. Nativists gave a new twist to the expression, "Not a Chinaman's chance."

Perhaps the crowning indignity came in 1892 with the

passage of the Geary Act, which oddly resembled southern slave codes abolished not thirty years before. This Act denied bail to the Chinese in habeas corpus cases and required all Chinese to obtain a certificate of eligibility to remain in the United States. If a Chinese person was arrested without such a certificate on his person, the burden of proof fell upon him to demonstrate his right to remain in the U.S. Much to the surprise of the Chinese Consul General and many Americans, the U.S. Supreme Court declared the Geary Act constitutional on the grounds of public interest and necessity.

Thus could a group of street-corner fanatics funnel into the political system and wield disproportionate power. Yet, despite the phenomenal success of the Workingmen's party, most nativists stood outside the political arena, manipulating public opinion and pressuring politicians behind a comfortable shield of anonymity. Their organizations had names—the American Protective Association, the Immigration Restriction League, and the Ku Klux Klan—but their members usually had no faces.

The American Protective Association was organized in Clinton, Iowa, in 1887 by Henry F. Bowers, who devoted his energies to ferreting out Catholic conspiracies. Bowers, a self-educated attorney from Baltimore, believed that he and many others had been deprived of a sound education by a Jesuit conspiracy against the public schools. Likewise, he felt that a Catholic conspiracy had undermined the reelection campaign of his friend, Mayor Arnold Walliker.

Fired by these imagined indignities, Bowers was quite successful, securing a membership for the A.P.A. in the Midwest and Rocky Mountain States. Alerted to the "Roman menace," new members swore never to cast ballots for Catholic candidates, never to employ Catholics when Protestants were available, and never to join Catholic workers on a picket line. The A.P.A. attracted disenchanted union members and laborers who felt particularly threatened by the competition of cheap Irish labor. It served its members as both a vehicle for political activity and as a fraternal order, with secret rituals, elaborate initiations, and a social activities program for members and their families. Though not a political party, the A.P.A. usually supported Republican candidates, which crippled its recruiting efforts in the white, Democratic South.

The A.P.A. faded away in the mid-1890s, but not before leaving behind a reputation for violence and exaggerated fears. A.P.A. members battled Catholics through the saloons of a Montana mining town during a day-long fracas in 1893. This incident was followed soon after by a shooting at a polling place in Kansas City, Missouri, during a municipal election. Rumors of full-scale warfare between the A.P.A. and Catholic groups were rampant in the early 1890s. The mayor of Toledo, Ohio, purchased a quantity of Winchester rifles with which Protestants could repel an anticipated Catholic invasion. It never materialized.

But by the second half of the 1890s, Irish and German Roman Catholics, once so frightening, had become prominent and crucial members of the electorate. Even a hint of anti-Catholicism became a liability for politicians with national aspirations. Yet, even as the membership of the somewhat aimless A.P.A. was trickling away, the much more sophisticated Immigration Restriction League was being organized in the east.

Founded by Boston patricians in 1894, the Immigration Restriction League set out to limit, but not completely end, immigration to the United States. On the rationale that open immigration allowed people of dubious background and limited capabilities into the U.S., the League proposed a literacy test as a means of insuring that those admitted would not become a burden on the society. Ostensibly, the League's proposal that every immigrant over sixteen years of age be literate in a language was not discriminatory. However, a higher proportion of northern and western Europeans had access to at least minimal education. Literacy tests, therefore, would effectively exclude a higher proportion of immigrants from southeastern Europe.

The League operated as a highly organized, extraordinarily tenacious lobbying group. Into the early 1900s, the literacy test was incorporated into Congressional bills and tacked on as rider amendments only to be vetoed or dropped. However, though League supporters might not publicly flaunt their xenophobia, they were influential individuals, roaming freely through the corridors of power. They kept the issue of a literacy requirement before the Congress until literacy tests for immigrants were established by Federal law during World War I.

Far from patrician and far from sophisticated was the Ku Klux Klan, which caught its second wind after the First World War and took up the cudgels for Americans who hoped to actively discourage immigrants from settling in their communities and competing for their jobs. Actually, the Klan was revived in 1915 by an ex-Methodist minister, Colonel Joseph Simmons, at a torchlight meeting on Georgia's Stone Mountain. The Colonel (an honorary title) hoped to profit by the opening of D. W. Griffith's movie, *Birth of a Nation,* by creating a fraternal lodge with secret rituals and a selective membership modeled on the old Klan of Reconstruction days depicted in the film. But the ashes of Reconstruction resentments proved difficult to stir and by 1920, Simmons had enrolled only 2,000 members. That year, the Colonel entered partnership with Edward Young Clark and Elizabeth Tyler, two public relations experts who had learned their trade in World War I Red Cross drives and now wished to apply their skills to a financially profitable venture. Under their leadership, the Klan flourished.

The "new" Klan branded the new immigrants, especially Roman Catholics and Jews, "subversives" directly threatening the American way of life. Klansmen led in a renewed call for an end to open immigration, derisively labeling the ideal of a melting pot, a "mess of sentimental pottage." Kenneth T. Jackson (*The Ku Klux Klan in the City, 1915–1930,* 1967) has argued that "the greatest source of Klan support came from rank and file nonunion blue-collar employees of large businesses and factories." A substantial minority of white-collar Klansmen were marginally successful independent businessmen, poorly paid clerks, and struggling dentists and chiropractors. A few unprincipled urban politicans also sought Klan support to bolster their sagging careers. All members of the Klan shared a desire to find an explanation, external to themselves, for the changes taking place in American society and for their lack of success in riding the crest of those changes. The new immigrants, so alien, so strange to life in America, seemed convenient scapegoats.

The Klan proudly claimed credit for the eventual passage of restrictive immigration legislation in 1921 and 1924, though other groups had agitated for the laws with equal fervor and great proficiency. Klansmen had supported local candidates who seemed sufficiently nativist and had pledged to work for the passage of restrictive laws. By and large, however, the Klan preferred public demonstration and catharsis to political manipulation and lobbying. White-robed, hooded Klansmen held public meetings, burned crosses, and committed occasional acts of violence such as the public flogging of immigrants or those who assisted the newcomers. Women's auxiliaries often joined in the marches and less violent attempts at intimidation.

Ironically, the final enactment of restrictive legislation seemed to dissipate the enthusiasm of organized nativists, no matter what their class or strategy. Immigration was all but choked off, yet the transformation of American society so repugnant to nativists proceeded. Throughout the era, immigrants actively resisted nativist verbal, legal, and physical assaults. These people who had traveled half-way around the globe refused to passively capitulate to nativist coercion.

III

The new immigrants battled discriminatory policies and legislation advocated by nativists with whatever weapons they could muster. Fewer in number, concentrated in the urban areas of the Northeast and Midwest, and unfamiliar with the intricacies of American institutions, immigrants usually sidestepped violence, turning instead to politics and pressure groups to counter the nativism increasingly widespread among Americans.

No major study has as yet chronicled the violent clashes of natives and newcomers perpetrated in the name of patriotism, nor have historians detailed immigrant resistance. However, the evidence available suggests that there was no collective immigrant response to nativist violence. Fear of further bloodshed and of deportation prompted most newcomers to choose discretion over retaliation. In the anthracite coalfields of Pennsylvania, there was frequent violence over union organization between miners and the ruffians hired by mine owners during the 1880s. However, most immigrant conflict was initiated by the Irish Catholic Molly Maguires against the Welsh and English owners they accused of exploitation. Slavic miners already in the field, perceiving their stay in America to be temporary, usually did not join the Mollies. Moreover, Irish contentiousness was often exaggerated by antiunionists who successfully hampered the growth of mine unionism by linking labor organization with terrorism in the public mind. According to labor historian Melvyn Dubofsky (*Industrialism and the American Worker, 1865–1920,* 1975), historians cannot agree whether or not the Industrial Workers of the World (IWW), organized in 1905, were "reformers or revolutionaries, political activists or apolitical organizers of the working class, industrial unionists or syndicalists." However, it is clear that many of those who initially joined the IWW, or Wobblies, were recently arrived unskilled immigrant laborers. Many of these were attracted by the concept of unionization along industrial, instead of craft, lines while others were drawn by the rhetoric of class war against capitalism. Though many Italians, Poles, and other east Europeans joined the Wobbies to strike against the Pressed Steel Car Company of McKees Rocks, Pennsylvania (1909), and textile strikes at Lawrence, Massachusetts (1912), and Paterson, New Jersey (1913), many immigrants left the union after the collapse of the twenty-two-week Paterson strike and few new immigrants ever took a leading role in Wobbly disorders.

Until the immigrants became naturalized voters and became accustomed to regular political participation, they had little clout in national politics. However, at the state and local levels, party bosses perceived the political potential of the new immigrants just as they had with earlier arrivals. In cities, urban bosses and their machines protected newcomers from nativist hostility, much of which was directed from state governments. State legislators representing districts with large numbers of native-born voters, who felt beleagured by an increasing population of alien Catholics and Jews, staunchly sponsored legislation to shape immigrant behavior, such as laws that restricted business and recreational activities on the Sabbath. These Sunday "blue laws" in New York were bitterly attacked by Democrats, especially those from Tammany Hall, as anti-immigrant in intent. In his famous discourse on urban politics in 1905, Tammany boss George Washington Plunkitt lashed out at the Republican legislature and governor: "We've got to eat and drink what they tell us to eat and drink, and have got to choose our time for eatin' and drinkin' to suit them. If they don't feel like takin' a glass of beer on Sundays, we must abstain. If they have not got any amusements up in their backwoods, we mustn't have none. We've got to regulate our whole lives to suit them. And then we have to pay their taxes to boot."

Jewish merchants who closed on Saturday and opened on Sunday were especially penalized by Sabbath laws. However, the pushcart peddlers and small shopkeepers on New York's Lower East Side soon learned that they could elude enforcement by "the brass button" (as New York's policemen were known) by paying five dollars in protection money to the cop on the beat. Generally the police, many of whom were Irish, were only too pleased to foil Protestant nativism and turn a profit besides.

By the 1920s, new immigrants were beginning to pound on the doors of America's most prestigious universities. Schools such as Columbia, Harvard, Yale, and Princeton responded by trying to install a dead-bolt lock. Wealthy private institutions, protected by influential friends and alumni, were impervious to the efforts of political bosses. Thus, leaders of organizations representing the newcomers had to use the subtler tools of public opinion and private persuasion to help immigrants and their children into the "old boy" network that emanated from major universities and led to positions of affluence and power. Often, however, they were little match for the white Anglo-Saxon Protestant establishment that opposed them.

One Harvard professor expressed the objections of numerous others when he complained that too many students were coming from outside the element from which the college had been chiefly recruited for three hundred years. In response, Harvard mounted a restrictive quota system in 1922 that especially affected the increasing number of east European Jews seeking admission. Revised admission questionnaires where designed to flag newcomers by asking "What change, if any, has been made since birth in your name or that of your father?" Louis Marshall of the American Jewish Committee led Jewish leaders in a public attack upon Harvard, arguing that such quotas were not only anti-Semitic in intent, but that any quotas based upon racial or religious criteria were "a calamity to the United States" as well as an elitist violation of a university's broader educational mission. When a special Faculty Committee appointed to investigate admissions policies reported on April 9, 1923, it recommended that Harvard repudiate earlier changes and retain a policy of "equal opportunity for all, regardless of race or religion" using "no novel process of scrutiny" to screen applicants. However, covert discrimination at Harvard and elsewhere continued, despite public declarations to the contrary. The immigrants and their supporters could not immediately overcome the powerful and prejudiced doorkeepers of America's elite institutions.

Some new immigrants responded to discriminatory policies in the U.S. by appealing to the governments of their native countries. Foremost among these were the Japanese. Unlike the Chinese, most of whom arrived in poverty, many Japanese came to America with sufficient capital to purchase farmland. Thus, the Japanese became efficient and productive growers in the United States while their homeland was achieving power and prestige in world affairs.

Predictably, the Japanese were viewed by many Americans as ambitious, aggressive, and a little too successful. Old fears of the "yellow peril" were stirred up, and racial nativists sounded the alarm. In 1905, the Asiatic Exclusion League was formed in San Francisco and succeeded in pursuading the city school board to restrict Japanese pupils to Chinatown schools. The Japanese community responded vigorously and attacked the spineless racism of California politicians. Many Japanese were well-educated and articulate. They petitioned the Japanese government to intervene with American authorities.

In 1906, only 93 of San Francisco's 25,000 pupils were Japanese. The Japanese government pointed out the absurdity of segregation to President Theodore Roosevelt. Hoping to avoid further escalation of the incident into an even greater diplomatic issue, Roosevelt pressured the school board into rescinding its directive. In return for Roosevelt's intervention, the Japanese government acceded to a "Gentlemen's Agreement" in 1907, by which it pledged to refuse exit visas to laborers wishing to emigrate to the United States.

Still, discrimination continued. Under the state law of 1913, California's Japanese residents were proscribed from owning land. Cleverly, the Japanese continued to acquire property by registering it under the names of their American-born children, when the courts failed to overturn this discriminatory state legislation.

The court of law was the logical forum for many of the immigrant's grievances against specific nativist activities. But, immigrants often found the legal system ponderous and judges unsympathetic, the procedures unfamiliar and officials intimidating. In a 1923 study, *The Immigrant's Day in Court,* Kate Holladay Claghorn charged, "The attitude of the immigrant toward the law and the courts, insofar as it is determined by the teaching of the lawyers and runners, will naturally be one of distrust and disrespect. . . . He is taught that bribery and influence are the regular methods of securing favorable decisions, that the extortionate fees he is called upon to pay are necessary to provide the expected bribes, that the immigrant has no chance before the American court without the aid of a lawyer skilled in a special kind of trickery." She advocated legal aid and education for the immigrants in their rights under the American legal system. The Sacco-Vanzetti case seemed to confirm Claghorn's assessment of the legal system. It demonstrated conclusively that new immigrants confronted a hostility so pervasive that it penetrated the very system of justice which the newcomers were being urged to respect and preserve. Nicola Sacco and Bartolomeo Vanzetti, two Italian immigrants who professed anarchist beliefs, were arrested in May 1920 and charged with the robbery and murder of a shoe company paymaster in South Braintree, Massachusetts. At their trial, the prosecutor was unable to conclusively demonstrate the pair's guilt. Nevertheless, nativist prejudices and a highly charged courtroom atmosphere resulted in a guilty verdict. Judge Webster Thayer of Worcester, who regarded the accused as "anarchist bastards," sentenced them to death by electrocution in July, 1921.

Protests and appeals postponed the execution date for six years. Intellectuals from around the world, including George Bernard Shaw, H. G. Wells, Albert Einstein, and Anatole France, protested the conviction and the questionable judicial procedures. Governor Alvin T. Fuller of Massachusetts, under heavy political pressure, formed an advisory committee which recommended that the executions proceed. On August 22, 1927, Sacco and Vanzetti were executed for a crime they may never have committed.

In 1927, some Americans applauded the execution as an appropriate response to the challenge that alien radicals posed to American law. Others regarded Sacco and Vanzetti as martyrs to the excesses of American capitalism. Louis Joughin and Edmund Morgan (*The Legacy of Sacco and Vanzetti,* 1948) wrote, "A feverish society discredited itself in the Sacco-Vanzetti case. Prejudice, chauvinism, hysteria, and malice were endemic to this country in the 1920s." The controversial nature of the case was formally acknowledged by Massachusetts Governor Michael Dukakis, who issued a proclamation on July 19, 1977, stating that Sacco and Vanzetti were not treated justly. A half century after their execution, a governor of Greek descent repudiated Brahmin injustice to two Italian immigrants.

The new immigrants could turn a deaf ear to the harangues of nativist demagogues such as Kearney, answer in kind the A.P.A.'s threats of violence, counter the political machinations of nativist state legislatures with their votes, and focus public attention on the hypocrisy of discriminatory liberal educators. However, newcomers and those who spoke for them could not halt the public groundswell for resticting immigration. World War I seeded the storm clouds. It sharply altered the relationship of Americans to the rest of the world. No longer did Americans feel isolated and safe, nestled between two great oceans. The world's problems had been handed a pair of water wings, and more than ever Americans felt vulnerable and suspicious. When nativists succeeded in turning that suspicion inward immediately after the war, the new immigrants were overwhelmed.

I V

Heightened sensitivity to foreigners stirred by World War I propaganda and postwar turmoil lent new authority to the restrictionist movement launched years earlier. But the immigrants, still too new to America, lacked the political and economic muscle to obstruct this drive for restriction.

The new immigrants in no way dominated the politics of states such as New York, Massachusetts, Pennsylvania, New Jersey, Illinois, and Ohio, though millions of newcomers lived elbow to elbow in their major cities. While immigrants swelled the representation to which those states were entitled, the newcomers were not eligible to vote until naturalization, nor were all of them equally enthusiastic about exercising the franchise once granted. As a result, the native born continued to superintend the Congressional and Presidential politics of their respective states. According to historian David Burner (*The Politics of Provincialism*, 1968), only the Great Depression of the 1930s kindled intense interest in national politics among the new immigrants.

Even those new immigrants who were eligible to vote and sufficiently motivated to go to the polls did not vote as a bloc. Voting analysts Samuel Lubell, David Burner, John Allswang, and Allan Lichtman have all explained that, prior to 1932, new immigrant groups expressed different party preferences in different cities. In the election of 1920, the new immigrant vote split severely over the controversial Wilson Peace Plan. Polish voters generally supported Wilson, while Italians and east European Jews joined older groups, such as the Irish and Germans, in voting Republican. The new immigrants were too divided politically to defeat nativism at the polls.

Nor did the immigrants wield sufficient economic power to stymie nativist intentions. New immigrant entrepreneurs were just gaining a foothold in the American economy and the majority of imigrants were blue collar. Organized labor, which voiced many of the economic grievances of immigrants, favored restriction. The American Federation of Labor and its president, Samuel Gompers, urged drastic reductions in immigration, fearing that a continued influx of unskilled workers from abroad would endanger the position of skilled craftsmen and drive down the wages of all American workers.

It took the antialien emotionalism generated by World War I to convert a persistent issue of political debate into a lightning rod for bipartisan support. World War I was a catalyst, not a cause of restrictionism. To generate enthusiasm for America's war effort, Woodrow Wilson sanctioned a massive propaganda campaign. The Committee on Public Information under George Creel encouraged a voluntary censorship program and employed the newest public relations techniques developed by businessmen to "sell" Americans the war and generate hatred toward the German foe. A staff of public relations experts in Washington and local patriots throughout the country printed pamphlets, arranged speeches and generally talked up "one hundred percent Americanism." In the spirit of the moment, sauerkraut was renamed "liberty cabbage" and 75,000 "Four Minute Men" were recruited by Creel's Committee to describe German atrocities to local community and church groups, urging them to buy Liberty Bonds. Soon, anyone and anything that smacked of foreign culture became suspect, and patriotism often degenerated into an ugly xenophobia that even the Creel Committee did not endorse. German language courses were removed from high school and college curricula. As part of a July 4th celebration, citizens of one Oklahoma town burned German-language books. And, in isolated outbursts of violence, German Americans were beaten, tarred, and feathered. In reaction, some families changed their German-sounding last names to avoid embarrassment or to protect their school-aged children from harrassment by classmates.

Most new immigrants realized that if they hoped to settle peacefully and live prosperously in the United States they must demonstrate their willingness to be "100% patriotic" and sacrifice for their new homeland. Therefore, many aliens not required to do so volunteered to fight in the armed services. Others worked in war industries and donated money or blood to the American Red Cross. Though many of the new immigrants were from eastern Europe, they cared little about the Austro-Hungarian Empire. Instead, east Europeans such as the Poles, Serbs, and Croations, hoped for self-determination for their ethnic groups after the war, a priority established by Woodrow Wilson among his Fourteen Points. Unfortunately, many Americans could not distinguish ties of blood and culture from ties of nationalism. Unable and unwilling to recognize the affectionate gratitude felt by most immigrants for the United States, these nativists maintained their suspicious vigil at the base of the flagpole.

During the war, proponents of the literacy test, such as the Immigration Restriction League, took advantage of fears that the United States would be innundated by unfit immigrants after the war. Though President Woodrow Wilson had vetoed a bill providing for such tests in 1915, the issue was reintroduced two years later as part of an omnibus bill that sought to tighten anti-radical provisions of the 1903 law and deny admission to the illiterate. In 1916, Democrats and Republicans hesitated to take any action that might forfeit the ethnic vote. However, immediately after the election, the Senate passed the omnibus bill. Wilson vetoed it, but this time immigration opponents capitalized on war-time hysteria to override the presidential veto in February 1917. Because there was a higher rate of illiteracy in southern and eastern Europe, the imposition of a literacy test amounted to a de facto quota system.

After the war, a bitterness that so many Americans had been killed or maimed in a war triggered by European ineptitude was compounded by the acute fear of communism. The spectre of the Russian Revolution, coupled with a postwar economic crisis, set off a major Red Scare. Fresh from battling the enemy abroad, Americans now looked to the subversive enemy within. The most likely culprit was the new immigrant.

American socialists had been vocal in their enthusiasm for early Bolshevik activities, especially redistribution of private property. Of course, most immigrants were not socialists and had little time for ideological debate of any sort. However, immigrants predominated in the membership of the Socialist party, so that newcomers, especially in eastern states, and political radicalism became inextricably entwined in the public mind.

After the war, there was an outburst of labor unrest as unions sought to secure their legitimacy as bargaining agents and win long delayed salary increases for their workers. The steel strike of 1919, textile strikes, and the strike of Boston's police force all lent a chaotic air to the postwar period. This economic turmoil and the remnants of wartime fears of subversion created a highly charged atmosphere. A series of bombings and attempted bombings in the spring of 1919 ignited the mixture. In April a bomb was sent to the mayor of Seattle. Another mailed to former senator Thomas W. Hardwick of Atlanta blew off the hands of Hardwick's maid. The Post Office intecepted thirty-four similar parcels addressed to such prominent businessmen as J. P. Morgan and John D. Rockefeller while newspaper headlines fueled the public imagination. In June, bombs exploded at approximately the same time in eight cities; one even shattered the windows of Attorney General A. Mitchell Palmer's home. Talk of radical conspiracies was rampant.

Attorney General Palmer and his eager young assistant, J. Edgar Hoover, branded the bombings and threats as the work of a radical element that they pledged to purge by whatever means necessary. Palmer thought he would find many of these radicals in the immigrant community. Palmer, according to historian Robert Muray (*Red Scare,* 1955), did not hesitate to use "insinuation, slander, character assassination, and smear . . . to compel conformity or enforce silence." Frightened middle-class Americans supported Palmer's excesses in the name of patriotism.

At first, agents from the Justice Department proceeded cautiously. Though 54 aliens were arrested in connection with a general strike in Seattle early in 1919, only 3 were actually deported. But, strikes and violence in the summer and fall of that year led to more aggressive efforts to expel radical aliens. On November 7, Palmer's agents undertook a country-wide raid against the Union of Russian Workers. Many hundreds were seized, though only 246 aliens were ultimately detained and judged to be deportable radicals. Raids against the Communist party and Communist labor parties in January 1919 netted more than 4,000 suspected radicals in thirty-three cities. More raids and more arrests followed, until the campaign reached its zenith in January, 1920. Though not all aliens arrested were deported, those taken into custody were often treated harshly, kept in makeshift jails with inadequate food and unsanitary conditions.

The hysteria passed almost as suddenly as it had begun. By early 1920, Americans were tiring of the witch-hunt. They began to realize that the Bolshevik threat to the U.S. had been greatly exaggerated by Palmer and Hoover. Moreover, the threat that communism posed in Europe appeared to be dwindling. The expulsion of Socialists legally elected to the New York State Legislature in 1920 frightened many Americans, who saw this patriotic hysteria hacking away at the institutions it purported to protect.

A calm settled over the country as the harrassment of new-comers subsided and Americans were distracted by a new source of entertainment, the radio, and the loss of an old one through prohibition. However, while many citizens retreated into sports and other nonpolitical diversions in pursuit of "normalcy," others, such as members of the Ku Klux Klan and the Immigration Restriction League, continued to lobby for quotas. This time their efforts bore fruit. Restrictionists won a narrow victory in Congress.

V

When postwar immigration rapidly rose to prewar levels, Senator William Paul Dillingham turned to the voluminous report his commission had released in 1911. The Dillingham Commission, a joint Senate-House committee, had published a forty-one volume report on every aspect of immigration to the United States. At the time of its release, the report denounced the new immigrants as less fit physically, intellectually, economically, and culturally than earlier American settlers and urged the passage of a literacy test and the consideration of immigration restriction based on nationality.

Senator Dillingham dredged up this idea and in 1920 drafted a bill that limited immigration according to a national quota system. The bill provided an annual quota for each immigrant group equal to 3 percent of the number of foreign-born of that group listed in the federal census of 1910. The House version that President Warren G. Harding signed into law in 1921 was scheduled to run for one year, but Congress renewed it twice.

Still, nativists complained that too great a number of Italians, Slavs, east European Jews, and Greeks were eligible for admission. The Johnson-Reed Act of 1924 addressed this problem by linking the number of immigrants allowed into the United States to the "percentage" of their group already here, rather than to a raw number. The law finally took effect in

1929, establishing a total quota of 153,714, excluding the Western Hemisphere and Asian nations, though most Asians were already excluded under earlier laws. All other nations were alloted a number of immigrants equal to their proportion of the U.S. population in 1920.

The law served its purpose. It permanently crippled the new immigration. Well over half of the quota was parceled out to Great Britain, Ireland, Germany, and the Scandinavian countries. While Britain was permitted an annual total of 65,361, only 5,803 Italians, 6,524 Poles, and 2,784 Russians were eligible for admission each year. Because the Western Hemisphere was not affected by the law, a small percentage of new immigrants managed to enter from Mexico, Canada, or Latin America. But the percentage was small, and no accurate figures are available.

The 1924 Act also delivered the coup de grace to Chinese immigrants. It excluded from immigration all aliens ineligible for citizenship. This provision effectively banned Chinese women from coming to the United States. The Act "virtually condemned the Chinese in the United States to a life of forced celibacy, bachelorhood, or trans-Pacific marriages," according to Betty Lee Sung. The ban was not lifted until 1952.

The new immigration was over. After forty years, nativists finally succeeded in persuading Congress to curb the entry of foreigners into the United States. Ironically, the new immigrants, so roundly accused by nativists of subverting American values and exercising undue influence over American institutions, had been unable to marshall sufficient political or economic influence to defeat restriction on the floor of Congress. The antialien feelings fed by World War I and its aftermath finally slammed "the golden door" celebrated by Emma Lazarus. Only the illegal route across the Canadian or Mexican border remained for the most desperate. Statistics are unreliable, but mingled among the French Canadians from the north and the Mexican laborers from the south were people from Europe and Asia who preferred the risks of illegal entry to turning back.

The new immigrants, steeled by adversity in their homelands, had not been deterred by the rhetoric of nativist rabble-rousers, the organized opposition of middle-class critics, or even the occasional violence of their native-born economic competitors. Immigrants vigorously protested exclusionary educational quotas. Their spokesmen and political allies denounced nativism and marshalled the votes of those already naturalized to battle restrictionist politicians. In the end, the fight for unrestricted immigration was lost in the face of overwhelming odds. The new immigrants were not yet sufficiently ensconced in the bastions of power and influence to do more than delay the coming of restriction. However, during the fray the newcomers served notice on their adversaries that few immigrants would be returning home. And those who chose to remain would continue to tussle with the native born, competing for resources and opportunities, determined to change America even as America was already changing them.

S I X

Conclusion

Social historian Herbert Gutman has suggested that the study of dependent American social classes, such as immigrants, must take into consideration how these groups interpreted and dealt with changing economic, social, and political patterns. Gutman looks to French existential philosopher Jean-Paul Sartre, who observed that, "The essential is not what 'one' has done to man, but what man does with what 'one' has done to him." In other words, it is only through examining the choices men and women made, by understanding "how their behavior affected important historical processes," that we can understand the human condition.

The immigrants who came to the United States in such numbers between 1880 and 1921 dramatically affected the shaping of the American population. By their very presence, these newcomers altered the economy, politics, and culture of the country. In turn, the immigrants were changed, in varying degrees, by the society they entered. The history of immigration to America can only be understood in light of "what was done" to a newcomer and native alike by this massive migratory movement. Immigrants were confronted with a series of options not even primarily of their own making, options not entirely to their taste. But it was the immigrants themselves who chose how to react; they were not simply the passive victims of large social forces. To portray the newcomers as hapless wayfarers not only robs them of their dignity, but obscures the part they played in creating a new character for America reflective of values, attitudes, and beliefs imported from around the world.

Some of the changes that the new immigrants effected in American society were the direct result of mere numbers. As immigrants jostled their way into America's labor force, they broadened the market for manufactured products, swelled the size of the cities, and eventually expanded the eligible electorate. Their presence required communities to increase the number and size of churches, schools, hospitals, and prisons. Municipal services from sewage removal to public lighting to playground construction had to be initiated to cope with the congestion. Vast armies of clergymen, policemen, sanitation workers, teachers, and social reformers were recruited to serve immigrant neighborhoods bursting at the seams with people and problems. The size and complexity of government increased, especially at municipal and county levels, as the crush of population propelled government into new roles and redefined old ones. Public servants became stewards of the American way as they frantically tried to force newcomers to adjust themselves to America rather than vice versa.

The contribution of so many varied immigrant cultures to the shape of the American national character is incalculable. Incalculable if only because that contribution is so elusive; often the influence of particular groups did not become apparent for a generation or so after arrival. As the immigrants learned English, they often left the imprint of their native tongue upon local linguistic patterns. In New York, Chicago, and Philadelphia, the English spoken in Polish, Italian, or Jewish enclaves filtered into the speech of nonimmigrant residents and of other ethnic groups. Similarly, the delicacies of Greece, southern Italy, Mexico, and China found their way onto menus throughout the country. More subtly, but even more importantly, the new immigrant groups left a legacy of social, moral, and religious values which their descendants have scattered throughout the population. The fierce loyalty of Italians to family, the yearning of east European Jews for scholarship and intellectual inquiry, the Asian emphasis on family and personal honor—all of these cultural imperatives have been woven into the American consciousness.

At times, cultural differences have promoted the creation of ethnic stereotypes and rivalries damaging to America's social harmony. Ancient antagonisms imported from the Old World have occasionally found their way into national politics, and foreign policy—especially as it relates to the countries of eastern Europe—rouses the slumbering loyalties of second- and third-generation immigrants. Sociologist Orlando Patterson (*Ethnic Chauvinism: The Reactionary Impulse,* 1977) has charged that these loyalties, camouflaged as ethnic pluralism, make a virtue of tribalism and segregation. He and others argue that only a new universalism can counteract the primitive parochialism of those who seek to preserve their old world customs in America at the cost of social cohesiveness and justice for the individual. However, others disagree. Sociologist Richard Gambino uses the term "creative ethnicity" to describe the predominately constructive rather than divisive role that new immigrant values contributed to American culture. According to Gambino, the varied heritages of new immigrants have been and can continue to be the inspiration for creative solutions to social problems which result from life in an affluent, geographically mobile, highly secular society in which individuality, material progress, and change often take precedence over community responsibility, order, and stability.

Many early critics were unable to see much value in the inundation of America by impoverished immigrants. Progressive reformer and labor historian John R. Commons believed it impossible to "unite into one people a congeries of races even more diverse than the resources and climates from which they drew subsistence." Commons claimed that the immigrants were doomed to failure in America because of their racial differences from the Anglo-Saxon Protestants who had fashioned the country's democratic society. He dismissed the possibility of assimilation, arguing that, "Races may change their religions, their forms of government, their modes of industry, and their languages, but underneath all these changes they may continue the physical, mental and moral capacities and incapacities which determine the real character of their religion, government, industry and literature."

Then, too, the immigrants wondered whether the United States would prove the appropriate place for them. Few professed unqualified happiness from the moment they arrived. Still, most did not accept Commons' fatalistic view that satisfaction would be forever elusive because they were innately different from their hosts. In a variety of languages—through memoirs, newspapers, songs, and tapes—new immigrants have left a record of their feelings about the gamble they took on life in America.

Despite the clash between their traditional ways and the demands of industrial America, many new immigrants regarded their decision to emigrate as fortuitous and harbored few regrets. One elderly European Jew wrote a letter to the Yiddish language *Jewish Daily Forward* in 1956 to discuss the past and reflect upon whether the good old days were really that good.

I still remember my home town in Russia, our simple little house lighted at night by a small kerosene lamp, the door thatched with straw nailed down with sackcloth to keep it warm in the winter. I still remember the mud in the streets of the town, so deep it was difficult to

get around; our fear of the Gentiles; and who can forget the poverty—
the times when there wasn't even a crust of bread?

While immigrant life was hardly easy, the writer recalled,
"When we came to New York, I thought we were entering
heaven." Now, years later, America seemed even better:

When I think of the modern conveniences we live with now, of the
wonderful inventions, achievements in various fields, that we enjoy,
and about the opportunities for everyone in this blessed country, I see
there's nothing to be nostalgic about.

Another east European Jewish immigrant living in Pittsburgh
told an oral historian during the 1970s, "I love my country and
the American flag. It gave me everything I ever dreamed of or
wanted. I was an American citizen, I made a living, raised my
son, gave him an education and saw him successful."

Of course, even immigrants devoted to their new country
often still loved their land of birth. Italian immigrant Constantine Panunzio proclaimed in his memoir, *Soul of an Immigrant,*
"I love thee America," but added, "I love thee, Italy, my native
land, with that mystic love with which men turn to their native
country and as Pilgrims to their shrine." Contemporary writer
Jerre Mangione, the child of immigrant Sicilian parents, details
in his memoir, *An Ethnic at Large,* an even greater ambiguity on
the part of Italian immigrants than Panunzio suggests. "Among
the Italians, more than one million men and women returned to
their native land after a brief sojourn. Those who chose to stay,
or had no other choice, planted roots in their adopted land by
having children, even while enduring the most excruciating hardships. The pain of uprooting themselves and trying to survive in
an alien land where they were not made to feel welcome eventually stopped hurting." Of himself, Mangione writes, "Rarely
did I encounter in the American world the sageness and love of
life I found among my Sicilian relatives; but theirs was an old
and static world which lacked the spirit of enterprise and faith in
the future that firmly attached me to that admixture of compatriots known as Americans."

A Bulgarian writer, Stoyan Christowe, evaluated his immigrant experience in a 1929 article, "Half an American." Though he chose to remain in America, even after a return visit to his homeland, Christowe still wondered, "Has the storm in my being lulled now that I have spent two-thirds of my life in a struggle for readjustment and adaptation?" His response was a qualified "yes." Fond of his new country, Christowe still could not feel thoroughly American: "I shall always be the adopted child, not the real son, of a mother that I love more than the one that gave me birth." More recently, a Polish immigrant, Valerie Kozaczka Demusz, of Dorchester, Massachusetts, returned to her native land. She was enchanted by the improvement she saw, but still decided, "No, I wouldn't want to live there." For her, America's prosperity had made immigration worthwhile. "But I'm telling you, the people have heaven on earth here, and they don't know it. I don't care—the poorest person lives like a millionaire after what I saw." She chose America over Poland because, "here are my roots. My children are born here."

Natsu Okuyana Ozawa, a Japanese immigrant, arrived in 1924. Alienated by American racism and discriminatory policies, she seriously considered returning to Japan. However, following World War II, she began to reassess her yearning for her homeland. "First I thought about going back to Japan, but we had two sons and they are pure citizens, see, so we better stay here. . . . No more always something doing of fright(ening) things or terrible things. I think in many ways very nice the people."

A standard greeting among Chinese immigrants was, "When are you going back to China?" recalls historian Betty Lee Sung. "As a young child, I remembered the adult conversation invariably revolved around going back to China. I gained a deep impression that China must be some sort of fairyland paradise." Years later, however, the conversation changed, according to Sung. "Nowadays, when I go to visit my mother's good friend, I hear no more talk about going back to China. This woman's children are grown and married, living in their own homes near her. Her life, her roots are deeply imbedded in

American soil. . . . She barely speaks a word of English, but her mind is now oriented to the thought that she is going to spend the rest of her days in the United States.''

To fully understand immigration, one must listen to these personal stories. Ultimately, history is not made by huddled masses, or even triumphant cavalcades, but by specific individuals, weighing options, making compromises, squaring shoulders, having a joke, and muddling through. Few illustrate with greater clarity than Nicholas Gerros, a Greek, that immigrants were not passive men and women, cowed by historical circumstance (June Namias, ed., *First Generation,* 1978). Gerros arrived from Macedonia as an impoverished youth in 1912. He built a $300,000 a year garment business and became prominent among Greek-Americans of northeastern Massachusetts. Did immigrants have choices? Were there compromises to be made? Certainly, according to Nicholas Gerros:

Don't forget, everything in your life, you decide, nobody else decides, unless they come with a gun at your head and say, 'Look decide my way or else.' Even then you got a choice either die or do what he says. You see what I mean? But most of the time you're free to decide. Everything else we bring as alibis that's all. They can't stop you from going on your own.

The new immigrants were merely those who looked at what was being done to them, decided to leave their homelands, chose America, and, upon arrival, could not be stopped.

Bibliographical Essay

The notion that the United States is a "nation of nations" has only recently become standard fare in most history classrooms. In an insightful essay, Rudolph Vecoli ("Ethnicity: A Neglected Dimension of American History" in Herbert Bass, ed., *The State of American History,* Chicago, 1970) contends that the neglect of immigration history resulted from a broader failure of American historians to write national history in the context of the "enormous diversity of race, culture, and religion that has characterized the American people." Until the 1960s, most American academicians believed that the vitality of the country's capitalist economy and its republican institutions quickly converted Europe's "wretched refuse" into a new people. Extensive discussion of diversity, then, seemed a senseless dwelling on a temporary condition.

If American historians resisted the notion of a heterogeneous America, this was consistent with their own homogeneity. Before 1920, most historians were old-stock white Anglo-Saxon Protestants, unsympathetic to immigrants and at times even given to a mild nativism in their scholarship. By the 1920s and 1930s, the children of the northern and western European immigrants were writing the history of their own groups, but scarcely noticed those from southern and eastern Europe, and Asia. Study of these people was left to social reformers such as sociologist Peter Roberts (*The New Immigrants: A Study of the Industrial and Social Life of Southeastern Europeans in America,* New York, 1912). Roberts drew upon his scholarly observations to support his advocacy of rapid assimilation of the newcomers. He told his readers, "I believe in the immigrant. He has in him the making of an American, provided a sympathetic hand guides him and smooths the path which leads to assimilation."

The great American historian Frederick Jackson Turner also observed the new immigration firsthand. In 1901, he wrote a series of newspaper articles which were filled with the stereotypes and clichés of the era. He found Italians "quick witted and supple in morals." Jews were "thrifty to disgracefulness, while their ability to drive a bargain amounts to genius." Nevertheless, Turner was aware of the need for more scholarly treatment of immigration. Even as he hailed the western frontier as a beneficent force for homogenization, Turner believed that the diversity of stocks "with their different habits, morals and religious doctrines and ideals . . . led to cross-fertilization and the evolution of a profoundly modified society."

Of Turner's students, only Marcus Lee Hansen made a lasting contribution to the study of the new immigration. The son of foreign-born parents, Hansen recognized that the peopling of America began in Europe and that it was as important to understand why some left and others stayed as to know why America was so attractive to immigrants. His seminal essay ("The History of American Immigration as a Field for Research," *American Historical Review*, XXXII, 1926-27, 500-518) called for the systematic collection and examination of "raw materials" on every aspect of immigrant life.

Not until Oscar Handlin's *The Uprooted* (Boston, 1951), did anyone focus on the new immigrant and his personal encounter with America. Handlin's almost poetic description of European peasants seeking better lives in the New World has been praised for its imagery, but more recently criticized for its inaccuracies, especially by Rudolph Vecoli in "Contadini in Chicago: A Critique of *The Uprooted,*" *Journal of American History*, LI (December 1964). Citing the experiences of the Italians who settled in Chicago, Vecoli persuasively refuted Handlin's profile, noting in particular that he fails to distinguish between different types of immigrants. Whatever its shortcomings, however, *The Uprooted* remains a milestone in the study of the new immigration, suggesting the need for greater specificity in defining the complex causes of European emigration in the late nineteenth and early twentieth centuries.

A decade after Handlin, Maldwyn Allen Jones published a valuable, comprehensive survey, *American Immigration* (Chicago, 1960). Jones recognized that different groups arrived at different times, but denied that these differences were significant, abandoning the traditional distinction between old and new immigrants. Jones, an Englishman, stressed the continuity of the larger social process of international migration. Another English scholar, Philip Taylor (*The Distant Magnet*, New York, 1971), also emphasized the similarities rather than the distinctions between the experiences of successive immigrant groups. The subtitle of Taylor's book, "European Emigration to the U.S.A.," accurately conveys the author's focus on the journey rather than the arrival and settlement. By preferring to emphasize the broad social forces that generated transoceanic migration, both Jones and Taylor neglect the distinctive quality of the experiences of each group and the major changes in

American society from the first great wave of immigration to the second.

That immigrants must be studied as distinct individuals as well as group members is suggested by Herbert Gutman in a provocative essay on the study of American "dependent" social classes. Gutman argues that immigrants—as well as slaves, poor free blacks, union and nonunion workers—must be understood in terms of how effectively they dealt with large social forces, making deliberate choices among perceived options. Though the options might be limited, the immigrant never was reduced to being merely a passive victim. Herbert Gutman, "Labor History and the 'Sartre Question'," *Humanities* 1 (September/October, 1980).

During the past fifteen years, historians and social scientists, many themselves descendants of new immigrants, have increased our knowledge of immigration. Even an many earlier works have appeared in new editions, fresh literature has emerged. I have found some volumes particularly informative in writing this book. On the Italians, there are several classics, Robert Foerster's *Italian Emigration of Our Times* (Cambridge, Mass., 1919, reprinted 1968) and John H. Mariano, *The Italian Contribution to American Democracy* (Boston, 1924, reprinted 1975). The latter is especially rich in its portrayal of Italian housing, education, occupations, and social welfare. Still very important for its concept of amoral familialism is Edward C. Banfield's study of small town Italian life in *The Moral Basis of a Backward Society* (New York, 1958). More recently there is Joseph Lopreato, *Italian Americans* (New York, 1970), and Alexander De Conde, *Half Bitter, Half Sweet: An Excursion into Italian-American History* (New York, 1971). Richard Gambino's *Blood of My Blood* (New York, 1975) is a rich anecdotal account of three generations of southern Italians. In *An Italian Passage: Immigrants to Three American Cities, 1890-1930* (New Haven, Conn., 1978), John W. Briggs presents a systematic study of Italian immigrant life in three midsized cities: Utica and Rochester, New York, and Kansas City, Missouri. Virginia

Yans-McLaughlin's *Family and Community: Italian Immigrants in Buffalo, 1880-1930* (Ithaca, N.Y., 1977) is a fine study of family and community relationships. The McLaughlin and Briggs volumes are especially valuable scholarly correctives for the distortions and exaggerations that often creep into colorful, more impressionistic studies. Andrew Rolle's *The Immigrant Upraised: Italian Adventurers and Colonists in An Expanding America* (Norman, Okla., 1968) is impressionistic, indeed, but this study of Italians who settled in rural America provides a nonurban perspective neglected by most other studies. Most current research centers around urban data, only adding to a serious gap in immigration scholarship. Not all immigrants were tenement-dwelling urbanites, nor was rural America the homogeneous domain of the white Anglo-Saxon Protestant.

There is a rapidly expanding literature on east European Jews. Moses Rischin's *The Promised City: New York's Jews, 1870-1914* (Cambridge, Mass., 1962), Ronald Sanders, *The Downtown Jews* (New York, 1969), Arthur S. Goren's *New York Jews and the Quest for Community: The Kehillah Experiment: 1908-1922* (New York, 1970), and most recently Irving Howe's *World of Our Fathers* (New York, 1976) all treat the Jews of the new immigration, but only those who settled in New York. Ande Manners in *Poor Cousins* (New York, 1972) provides a broader picture of the conflict between the German and Russian Jews, but there is still a need for scholarly studies of the east European Jewish experience in midsized cities and smaller communities. An excellent effort in this direction is Marc Lee Raphael's *Jews and Judaism in a Midwestern Community: Columbus, Ohio, 1840-1875* (Columbus, Ohio, 1979).

Other new immigrant groups have received even less attention than the southern Italians and east European Jews. Two old but still useful volumes on the Poles are Paul Fox, *The Poles in America* (New York, 1922, reprinted 1970), and W. I. Thomas and F. Znaniecki, *The Polish Peasant in Europe and America,* 2 volumes (New York, 1958). The best volumes on Polish institutions in America are Joseph Wytrawal, *America's Polish Heritage: A Social History of the Poles in America* (Detroit, 1961), and *The Poles in America* (Minneapolis, Minn., 1969). An excellent overview in Helen Znaniecki Lopata, *Polish Americans: Status and Competition in an Ethnic Community* (Englewood Cliffs, N.J., 1976).

There have also been a few studies of other central and eastern European groups. The best of these are Emily Balch, *Our Slavic Felow Citizens* (New York, 1910, reprinted 1969); Wasyl Halich, *Ukrainians in the United States* (Chicago, 1937, reprinted 1970); Emil Lengyel, *Americans From Hungary* (Philadelphia, 1948, reprinted 1975); George J. Prpic, *Croatian Immigrants in America* (New York, 1971); and Jerome Davis, *The Russian Immigrant* (New York, 1922, reprinted 1969).

On Mediterranean immigrants, the undisputed authority on Greeks is Theodore Saloutos, *The Greeks in the United States* (Cambridge, Mass., 1963). A more concise but thoroughly useful volume is Charles C. Moskos, Jr.'s *Greek Americans: Struggle and Success* (Englewood Cliffs, N.J., 1980). Armenians are treated in Aram Yeretizian, *A History of Armenian Immigration to America with Special Reference to Los Angeles* (San Francisco, 1974). Though more of a personal memoir, Michael J. Arlen's *Passage to Ararat* (New York, 1975) is a poignant account of the Armenian experience and the issue of assimilation. On the Arabs, see Habib Ibrahim Katibah, *Arab-Speaking Americans* (New York, 1946). The great need for studies of the Arab immigrant experience in the period 1880–1921 will no doubt be met as universities increasingly receive endowments from Arab nations to establish Semitic studies programs and to finance research.

Literature on the Asian immigrant experience is steadily growing. An excellent volume on the Chinese is Jack Chen, *The Chinese of America* (San Francisco, 1980). Still useful are Mary B. Coolidge, *Chinese Immigration* (New York, 1909, reprinted 1969), Jack Chen, *The Chinese of America* (New York, 1980), and Betty Lee Sung, *Mountain of Gold* (New York, 1967). On the Japanese, Yamato Ichihashi's volume written in response to the critics of Japanese immigration is still important, *Japanese in the United States* (Stanford, 1932, reprinted 1969). More recent are works which combine historical and sociological approaches such as Harry Kitano, *Japanese Americans: The Evolution of a Subculture* (Englewood Cliffs, N.J., 1969) and William Petersen, *Japanese Americans: Oppression and Success* (New York, 1971).

Studies of new immigrant groups from other countries in the Americas include, on the French Canadians: Marcus Lee Hansen, *The Mingling of the Canadian and American Peoples* (New Haven, Conn., 1940, reprinted 1970); Iris Podea, "Quebec to 'Little Canada': The Coming of the French Canadians to New England in the Nineteenth Century," *New England Quarterly,* 23 (Fall 1950); George F. Theriault, "The Franco-Americans of New England," in Mason Wade, ed. *Canadian Dualism* (Toronto, 1960); Maurice Violette, *The Franco Americans* (New York, 1976). Recent interest in illegal aliens from Mexico has spurred scholarship on that group. The best recent overviews are Rodolfo Acuña, *Occupied America: The Chicano Struggle Toward Liberation* (San Francisco, 1972) and Matt S. Meier and Feliciano Rivera, *The Chicanos: A History of Mexican Americans* (New York, 1972). Several older but still useful volumes are Manuel Gamio, *Mexican Immigration and the United States* (Chicago, 1930, reprinted 1969) and *The Mexican Immigrant: His Life Story* (Chicago, 1931, reprinted 1969). Less scholarly, but always readable is Carey McWilliams, *North from Mexico: The Spanish People in the United States* (Philadelphia, 1948).

The general framework of this volume was shaped by those scholars who trained their attention on specific phases in the new immigrant's metamorphosis from alien to American. Taylor's *Distant Magnet* is still the most thorough book on the social conditions that stimulated emigration. All U.S. government statistics on the dimensions of the new immigration to this country are suspect because of inconsistent, even haphazard collection procedures. As reliable as any are those compiled in Walter F. Wilcox, ed., *International Migrations,* 2 volumes (New York, 1929). Though aimed at a popular rather than a scholarly readership, Maldwyn Allen Jones' *Destination America: 1815–1914* (New York, 1976) describes the hardship of the new immigrants' journey to America and compares it to that experienced by earlier travelers. William Tefft and Thomas Dunne, *Ellis Island* (New York, 1971) offer a valuable portrait of immigration inspection procedures, and, recently, the immigrants' own accounts of the admission process has been compiled by David M. Brownstone, Irene M. Franck and Douglas L. Brownstone in *Island of Hope, Island of Tears* (New York, 1979). Immigration administration, especially on Ellis Island is the subject of Thomas Monroe Pitkin's *Keepers of the Gate: A History of Ellis Island* (New York, 1975). Pitkin extends his study to include a useful account of the restriction controversy in the twentieth century.

The new immigrant's entry into the socioeconomic structure of his new homeland has become a topic in the larger historiographical debate over mobility. Though it does not deal with the new immigrants at all, every student of socioeconomic mobility must begin with Stephan Thernstrom's *Poverty and Progress: Social Mobility in a Nineteenth Century City* (Cambridge, Mass., 1964), which rescued the methodology of the social historian from speculation and impressionism. In this book as in subsequent works by other historians, mobility is defined occupationally. Thernstrom's second volume traces both new immigrants and native-born in Boston over several generations, *The Other Bostonians: Poverty and Progress in the American Metropolis, 1880–1970* (Cambridge, Mass., 1969). Taking their cue from Thernstrom, scholars of the new immigration have applied social scientific methods to the exploration of occupational mobility. Humbert Nelli studied a single group in one city in *Italians in Chicago, 1880–1930: A Study of Ethnic Mobility* (New York, 1970). Others have compared different new immigrant groups residing in the same locale, Josef Barton, *Peasants and Strangers: Italians, Rumanians, and Slovaks in an American City, 1890–1950* (Cambridge, Mass., 1975) and Thomas Kessner, *The Golden Door: Italian and Jewish Immigrant Mobility in New York City, 1880–1915* (New York, 1977). I have been especially influenced by James A. Henretta's contention that some new immigrants placed higher priority on noneconomic values such as close family ties and community involvement than on economic success. See Henretta's penetrating critique, "The Study of Social Mobility: Ideological Assumptions and Conceptual Bias," *Labor History,* 18 (Spring, 1977), 165-178.

Much remains to be known about how the new immigrants selected their homes and jobs and pursued the good life in America. Edward P. Hutchinson *Immigrants and Their Children, 1850-1950* (New York, 1956, new edition 1976) traces the migration and occupational patterns of European ethnic populations across the United States over several generations. Recently, a study of the Polish community in Philadelphia by Caroline Golab, *Immigrant Destinations* (Philadelphia, 1977), has demonstrated most persuasively that industrial patterns more than any other variable account for new immigrant migration patterns within the United States. Historical studies of new immigrant entrepreneurial activity are still sparse. An excellent comparative study of Asian immigrants and American blacks is by sociologist Ivan H. Light, *Ethnic Enterprise in America: Business and Welfare Among the Chinese, Japanese and Blacks* (Berkeley, Calif., 1972). He argues that voluntary associations were critical in enabling newcomers to amass capital for investment and to sustain infant ethnic enterprises.

The new immigrant served as a catalyst in the growth of the labor movement. The classic histories of the labor movement are John R. Commons et al., *History of Labor in the United States,* 4 volumes (New York, 1918-1935) and Selig Perlman's *A Theory of the Labor Movement* (New York, 1928). Most useful in specifying the influence of each new immigrant group upon the movement were: Melech Epstein, *Jewish Labor in the United States, 1882-1952,* 2 volumes (New York, 1950-1953); Edwin Fenton, *Immigrants and Unions, A Case Study: Italians and American Labor* (New York, 1975); Victor Greene, *The Slavic Community on Strike: Immigrant Labor in Pennsylvania Anthracite* (South Bend, Ind., 1968); and Gerald Rosenblum, *Immigrant Workers: Their Impact on American Labor Radicalism* (New York, 1973). The latter two, especially, discuss the old-world experiences and fears at the root of new immigrants' initial hesitation to be militant or even join unions.

In the immigrant family, women as well as men worked. However, there have been few books written about these working women, or for that matter, any aspect of the new immigrant woman's life. Among the older works still useful are Caroline Manning, *The Immigrant Woman and Her Job* (Washington, D.C., 1930, reprinted 1970); Elizabeth Beadsley Butler, *Woman and Her Trades: Pittsburgh, 1907-1908* (New York, 1909, reprinted 1969); Louise Odencrantz, *Italian Women in Industry* (New York, 1919); Bessie Pekotsky, *The Slavic Immigrant Woman* (Cincinnati, Ohio, 1925, reprinted 1971); Grace Abbott, *The Immigrant and the Community* (New York, 1917, reprinted 1971). More recently, scholarship in this field has been stimulated by the women's rights movement. Among the better efforts are Cecyle S. Needle, *America's Immigrant Women* (Boston, 1975); Charlotte Baum et al., *The Jewish Woman in America* (New York, 1976); and the essays on Italian immigrant women in Betty Boyd Caroli et al., eds., *The Italian Immigrant Woman in North America* (Toronto, 1978). Most impressive is Leslie Woodsock Tentler's *Wage-earning Women: Industrial Work and Family Life in the United States, 1900-1930* (New York, 1979). Tentler places immigrant women and the immigrant family in the larger context of industrial America, a difficult but crucial task. *Immigrant Women* (Philadelphia, 1981), a documentary study edited by Maxine Schwartz Seller, is a valuable anthology of memoirs, diaries, oral histories, and fiction to which scholars can turn. Especially useful were the essays in Charles H. Mindel and Robert W. Habenstein, eds., *Ethnic Families in America: Patterns and Variations* (New York, 1976). The introductory essay is an excellent synthesis of what is known and what needs to be known about the differing patterns of family life among ethnic groups in the United States.

In this book the subject of Americanization has been divided into three categories: schools, social reform, and politics. The debate among historians and educators over the role of the public school in the immigrant community waxed hot during the past decade. Radical scholars such as Colin Greer, *The Great School Legend: A Revisionist Interpretation of American Public Education* (New York, 1972) have argued that schools were weapons of social control used by the American establishment to control the poor, including immigrants, and inhibit their progress, thereby preserving the existing class structure. I have found such arguments unpersuasive, though there can be little doubt that schools were vehicles of assimilation and that individual new immigrant groups had very different educational experiences, often a function of differing cultural values and expectations. The most useful recent volume describing the controversy over public schools is Diane Ravitch, *The Great School Wars: New York City, 1805-1973: A History of the Public Schools as Battlefields of Social Change* (New York, 1974). The focus now needs to be shifted to individual immigrant groups. A classic is Leonard Covello, *The Social Background of the Italo-American School Child* (Totowa, N.J., 1967). While much is often made over the success of Jewish children compared to those of otper groups, there is still no major historical study of the Jewish experience in the public schools. Some useful volumes in exploring the role of education in the Americanization process are: Edward Hartmann, *The Movement to Americanize the Immigrant* (New York, 1948); Lawrence A. Cremin, *The Transformation of the School: Progressiveness in American Education, 1876-1957* (New York, 1961); David Tyack, *The One Best System: A History of American Urban Education* (Cambridge, Mass., 1974); Gerd Korman, *Industrialization, Immigrants, and Americanizers: Two Views From Milwaukee, 1866-1921* (Madison, 1967); and Robert Carlson, *The Quest for Conformity: Americanization Through Education* (New York, 1975). The best volume on the immigrants' efforts to preserve their own language is Joshua Fishman and Vladimir Nahirny, *Language Loyalty in the United States* (The Hague, 1966).

Social problems confronting newcomers, especially those encountered in urban areas, have been the subject of several excellent sociological studies, including William Foote Whyte, *Street Corner Society: The Social Structure of an Italian Slum*

(Chicago, 1943) and Herbert Gans, *The Urban Villagers: Group and Class Life of Italian Americans* (Glencoe, Ill., 1962). Organized crime is thoughtfully treated by Humbert Nelli, *The Business of Crime: Italians and Syndicate Crime in the United States* (New York, 1976), while the problems of new immigrants dealing with a strange and awesome legal system are studied by Kate Claghorn, *The Immigrant's Day in Court* (New York, 1923, reprinted 1969).

Assistance was rendered the immigrants by native-born reformers, the newcomers' own churches and associations, and the local apparatus of American political parties. Allen F. Davis finds settlement workers less paternalistic than many Progressive reformers in *The Social Settlements and the Progressive Movement, 1890–1914* (New York, 1967). However, a more crisp, hard-hitting critique of reformers is to be found in the more recent volume by Paul McBride, *Culture Clash: Immigrants and Reformers, 1880–1920* (San Francisco, 1975). Paul Boyer's *Urban Masses and Moral Order in America, 1820–1920* (Cambridge, Mass., 1978) effectively places Progressive reform into the broader historical context of efforts to tame the cities. The sympathetic, but often condescending attitudes of reformers toward immigrants can be detected firsthand in Jacob Riis, *How the Other Half Lives* (New York, 1890, reprinted many times); *The Battle with the Slums* (New York, 1902, reprinted 1969); John Spargo, *The Bitter Cry of the Children* (New York, 1908, reprinted 1969); Lillian Wald, *The House on Henry Street* (New York, 1915, reprinted 1969); Jane Addams, *Twenty Years at Hull House* (New York, 1910, reprinted 1961); and Robert Hunter, *Poverty* (New York, 1904).

Volumes which effectively treat the new immigrants' voluntary associations are greatly needed. The few worth consulting are John Daniels, *America Via the Neighborhood* (New York, 1920, reprinted 1971); Boris Bogen, *Jewish Philanthropy: An Exposition of the Principles and Methods in Jewish Social Services in the United States* (New York, 1917, reprinted 1969); and Victor Greene's *For God and Country: The Rise of Polish and Lithuanian Ethnic Consciousness in America, 1860–1910* (Madison, 1975). The YIVO Institute for Jewish Research is engaged in a project to collect the papers of *landsmanschaftn*.

Protestant efforts to reach newcomers are outlined in Carroll-Smith Rosenberg, *Religion and the Rise of the American City: The New York City Mission Movement, 1812-1870* (Ithaca, N.Y., 1971). These missions were already operating by the time new immigrants arrived in the 1880s, serving as challenges to Catholic and Jewish clergymen. See Aaron Abell, *American Catholicism and Social Action: A Search for Social Justice, 1865-1900* (Garden City, N.Y., 1960). Also see the excellent essays on the Poles, Slovaks, east European Jews, Czechs, and Armenians in Randall M. Miller and Thomas D. Mazrik, eds., *Immigrants and Religion in Urban America* (Philadelphia, 1977). Some scholars contend that the Catholic Church paid less attention to the new immigrants than it had to the Irish in an earlier era. A very persuasive case is made in Richard M. Linkh, *American Catholicism and European Immigrants, 1900-1924* (Staten Island, N.Y., 1975).

Urban political machines that sought to barter assistance for the votes of the newcomers have been the focus of a literature too extensive to cite here. The greatest insight into the urban political machine can be found in the words of Tammany boss G. W. Plunkitt as recorded by William L. Riordan and edited by Arthur Mann, *Plunkitt of Tammany Hall* (New York, 1963). The most erudite theoretical discussion of how the machine functioned can be found in Robert K. Merton's *Social Theory and Social Structure* (Glencoe, Ill., 1957). Several fine historical treatments of bosses are Seymour Mandelbaum's *Boss Tweed's New York* (New York, 1965) and Alex Gottfried, *Boss Cermak of Chicago: A Study of Political Leadership* (Seattle, 1962). New evidence uncovered by Leo Hershkowitz suggests that Boss Tweed may not have been quite the thief he is reputed to have been, *Tweed's New York: Another Look* (Garden City, 1977). Other studies are needed, however, to determine whether local party machinery actually fostered assimilation among the new immigrants or preserved ethnic insularity and neighborhood ties.

The best contemporary critique of machine politics is Lincoln Steffens, *The Shame of the Cities* (New York, 1904). J. Joseph Huthmacher attacks the notion that the new immigrants were merely manipulated by politicians and suggests that ethnic communities were actually the source of reform, *Senator Robert F. Wagner and the Rise of Urban Liberalism* (New York, 1968). The actual voting behavior of new immigrant communities at the municipal level has yet to be exhaustively analyzed. A pioneering effort is Arthur Goren, "A Portrait of Ethnic Politics: The Socialists and the 1908 and 1910 Congressional Elections on the East Side," *Publication of the American Jewish Historical Society,* 50 (March, 1961), 202–238. Recent studies include Edward R. Kantowicz, *Polish-American Politics in Chicago, 1888–1940* (Chicago, 1975); Thomas Henderson, *Tammany Hall and the New Immigrants: The Progressive Years* (New York, 1976); and the essays in Angela T. Pienkos, ed., *Ethnic Politics in Urban America: The Polish Experience in Four Cities* (Chicago, 1978).

Many political scientists and ethnocultural political historians regard the new immigrant vote as a variable of increasing significance in national politics in the twentieth century. See Samuel Lubell's *The Future of American Politics* (New York, 1951); John Allswang, *A House for All People: Chicago's Ethnic Groups and Their Politics, 1890–1936* (Lexington, K.Y., 1971); Thomas J. Pavlak, *Ethnic Identification and Political Behavior* (San Francisco, 1976), and Allan J. Lichtman, *Prejudice and the Old Politics: The Presidential Election of 1928* (Chapel Hill, N.C., 1979). Louis Gerson treats the impact of ethnic communities on foreign policy after 1900 in *The Hyphenate in Recent American Politics and Diplomacy* (Lawrence, Kan., 1964).

On assimilation, see Milton M. Gordon, *Assimilation in American Life: The Role of Race, Religion and National Origins* (New York, 1964). The classic defense of cultural pluralism is Horace M. Kallen, *Culture and Democracy in the United States* (New York, 1924). Will Herberg set forth a triple melting-pot model in *Protestant, Catholic, and Jew* (New York, 1955, reprinted 1960), but I found the "pluralist integration" model described by John Higham in *Send These to Me* the most persuasive account of the new immigrants' relationship to American society.

The ascension of a new ethnic awareness has stimulated an abundance of works that place the new immigrants into a larger ethnic mosaic of America, alongside native Americans (Indians), blacks, and "old" immigrant groups. The most thorough and comprehensive of these books is *To Seek America* (Englewood, N.J., 1977) by Maxine Schwartz Seller, though Leonard Dinnerstein and David Riemers' *Ethnic Americans: A History of Immigration and Assimilation* (New York, 1975) treats the immigrants in greater detail. The fatal flaw in all such efforts, however, is that the distinctiveness of specific groups gets lost in the shuffle as the authors rush on from one to the next.

Nativism and less ideological forms of anti-immigrant prejudice have generated a rich and diverse lierature. Still, the classic historical work on nativism in the period after the Civil War is John Higham, *Strangers in the Land: Patterns of American Nativism, 1860–1925* (New Brunswick, N.J., 1955). A more recent volume of essays deals with anti-Semitism and Higham's latest thoughts about ethnic relations, *Send These To Me: Jews and Other Immigrants in Urban America* (New York, 1975). The Popularity that nativist writers enjoyed at the turn of the century makes it useful to consult their writings to understand the concerns they had about the impact of the new immigration on American society. See Edward Alsworth Ross, *The Old World in the New* (New York, 1914); Madison Grant, *The Passing of the Great Race* (New York, 1916); Lothrop Stoddard, *The Rising Tide of Color* (New York, 1920). The classic nativist assault on Roman Catholicism in the post–Civil War period is Rev. Josiah Strong, *Our Country, Its Possible Future and Its Present Crisis* (New York, 1885). Nativist assertions of the biological inferiority of immigrants did not go unanswered. See Franz Boas, *Changes in Bodily Form of Descendants of Immigrants in Reports of the Immigration Commission* (61 Cong., 2 Sess.,

Senate Document No. 208, Washington, D.C., 1911) and *Race and Democratic Society* (New York, 1945).

Some recent volumes that examine the defensive reactions of native Americans are: Morton Rosenstock, *Louis Marshall: Defender of Jewish Rights* (Detroit, 1965); Leonard Dinnerstein, *The Leo Frank Case* (New York, 1968); Marcia Graham Synott, *The Half-Opened Door: Discrimination and Admissions at Harvard, Yale and Princeton, 1900-1970* (Westport, Conn., 1979); Robert K. Murray, *Red Scare: A Study in National Hysteria, 1919-1920* (Minneapolis, Minn., 1955); Donald Kinzer, *An Episode in Anti-Catholicism: The American Protective Association* (Seattle, 1964); and Stuart Creighton Miller, *The Unwelcome Immigrant: The American Image of the Chinese, 1785-1882* (Berkeley, Calif., 1969). Material on the Ku Klux Klan abounds, but the best volume on anti-immigrant activities is Kenneth T. Jackson, *The Ku Klux Klan in the City, 1915-1930* (New York, 1967). Still the best volume on the cultural milieu in which the Sacco-Vanzetti case occurred is Edmund M. Morgan and Louis Joughin, *The Legacy of Sacco and Vanzetti* (New York, 1948, reprinted 1977). See also Osmond Fraenkel, *The Sacco-Vanzetti Case* (New York, 1931); Herbert B. Ehrmann's *The Case That Will Not Die: Commonwealth vs. Sacco and Vanzetti* (Boston, 1969) sets forth the legal issues most lucidly.

Almost unconsidered is the relationship between new immigrant groups. A useful volume that addresses intergroup tensions is Ronald H. Bayor, *Neighbors in Conflict: The Irish, Germans, Jews, and Italians of New York City, 1919-1941* (Baltimore, 1978).

The contemporary debate over the value of ethnic loyalties, the legacy of immigration is the subject of some provocative volumes, including Michael Novak, *The Rise of the Unmeltable Ethnics* (New York, 1971); Orlando Patterson, *Ethnic Chauvinism: the Reactionary Impulse* (New York, 1977); Howard F. Stein and Robert F. Hill, *The Ethnic Imperative* (Philadelphia, 1977); and Stephen Steinberg *The Ethnic Myth: Race, Ethnicity and Class in America* (New York, 1981).

The basic policies and legislation on American immigration that affected the new immigrants are set forth succinctly and clearly in Marion T. Bennett, *American Immigration Policies: A History* (Washington, D.C., 1963), and Robert A. Divine, *American Immigration Policy, 1924-1952* (New Haven, Conn., 1957, reprinted 1972).

The new immigrants tell their own story best. The most informative accounts of the newcomers' motives, objectives, and reflections cited throughout the text, especially in the conclusion, are from such immigrant memoirs as: Louis Adamic, *Laughing in the Jungle* (New York, 1932), the odyssey of a Yugoslavian lad; *From Plotzk to Boston* (Boston, 1899) and *The Promised Land* (Boston, 1912) by Mary Antin, a Russian Jew who became a writer in America; *The Soul of an Immigrant* (New York, 1921) by Italian minister and social worker Constantine Panunzio; *From Immigrant to Inventor* by Serbian physicist Michael Pupin (New York, 1922); *Rosa, The Life of an Italian Immigrant* (Minneapolis, Minn., 1970), the chronicle of an Italian woman as told to Marie Hall Ets; *Bread Upon the Waters* (New York, 1944), by Rose Pesotta, the Russian Jew who served four times as the I.L.G.W.U.'s vice president. Jewish immigrants tell of their problems in their letters to the *Jewish Daily Forward's* editor Abraham Cahan. Isaac Metzker, ed., *A Bintel Brief* (New York, 1971). *The Education of Abraham Cahan* (Philadelphia, 1969), the autobiography of a journalist and advocate of the Jewish immigrant, is a valuable source. Irving Howe and Kenneth Libo have made available many of the valuable documents they cited in *World of Our Fathers* in *How We Lived: A Documentary History of Immigrant Jews in America, 1880-1930* (New York, 1979). Several other collections are: Moses Rischin, ed., *Immigration and the American Tradition* (Indianapolis, 1976); Stanley Feldstein and Lawrence Costello, eds., *The Ordeal of Assimilation: A Documentary History of the White Working Class, 1930s to the 1970s* (Garden City, N.Y., 1974); and Salvatore La Gumina and Frank J. Cavaioli, eds., *The Ethnic Dimension in American Society* (Boston, 1974).

Since the late 1970s, the emphasis on ethnicity and the re-discovery of one's roots has yielded valuable oral histories. Volumes of testimony which I found especially useful are: *By Myself I'm a Book: An Oral History of the Immigrant Jewish Experience* prepared by the Pittsburgh Section of the National Council of Jewish Women (Waltham, Mass., 1972); June Namias' fine compilation or oral histories, *First Generation* (Boston, 1978); and Joan Morrison and Charlotte Fox Zabusky, *American Mosaic: The Immigrant Experience in the Words of Those Who Lived It* (New York, 1980). Many more such works are needed. The publication of practical guides to doing family history is encouraging other new immigrants and their children to pursue the past. Among the best are Jim Watts and Allen F. Davis, *Generations: Your Family in Modern American History* (New York, 1974); Passi Rosen-Bagewitz and Menda Novek, *Shiloah: Discovering Jewish Identity Through Oral Folk History:* (New York, 1976); Allan J. Lichtman, *Your Family History: How to Use Oral History, Personal Family Archives and Public Documents to Discover Your Heritage* (New York, 1978). The best practical guide to oral history is Ellen Robinson Epstein and Rona Mendelsohn, *Record and Remember: Tracing Your Roots Through Oral History* (New York, 1978).

INDEX